KZ

Law of Nations

Library of Congress Classification
2012

Prepared by the Policy and Standards Division
Library Services

LIBRARY OF CONGRESS
Business Enterprises
Cataloging Distribution Service
Washington, D.C.

This edition cumulates all additions and changes to Class KZ through Weekly List 2011/25, dated October 17, 2011. Additions and changes made subsequent to that date are published in lists posted on the World Wide Web at

<http://www.loc.gov/aba/cataloging/classification/weeklylists/>

and are also available in *Classification Web*, the online Web-based edition of the Library of Congress Classification.

Library of Congress Cataloging-in-Publication Data

Library of Congress.
Library of Congress classification. KZ. Law of nations / prepared by the Policy and Standards Division, Library Services.
p. cm.
"This edition cumulates all additions and changes to Class KZ through Weekly List 2011/25, dated October 17, 2011. Additions and changes made subsequent to that date are published in lists posted on the World Wide Web ... and are also available in Classification Web, the online Web-based edition of the Library of Congress Classification"--T.p. verso.
Includes index.
ISBN 978-0-8444-9537-8 -- ISBN 0-8444-9537-9
1. Classification--Books--International law. 2. Classification, Library of Congress. I. Library of Congress. Policy and Standards Division. II. Title. III. Title: Law of nations.
Z696.U5K77 2012 025.4'6341--dc23 2012000841

For sale by the Library of Congress Cataloging Distribution Service,
101 Independence Avenue, S.E., Washington, DC 20541-4912.
Product catalog available on the Web at **www.loc.gov/cds**.

PREFACE

The first edition of subclass KZ, Law of Nations, was published in 1997 as an experimental draft edition. Together with its companion subclass, JZ, International relations, it replaced the former subclass JX, International law. A revised 1998 edition of KZ resolved various issues identified by the Library of Congress and other institutions during the first year of application of the schedule. KZ was again published in 2007, cumulating additions and changes since 1998. This 2011 edition includes additions and changes since 2007 and contains a new development for international criminal law in KZ7000-KZ7500. The focus of the development is on the International Criminal Court (ICC). The new numbers for the ICC (KZ7250-KZ7490) include all subjects and doctrines relating to the ICC, as well as its reports, digests, and pleadings.

Classification numbers or spans of numbers that appear in parentheses are formerly valid numbers that are now obsolete. Numbers or spans that appear in angle brackets are optional numbers that have never been used at the Library of Congress but are provided for other libraries that wish to use them. In most cases, a parenthesized or angle-bracketed number is accompanied by a "see" reference directing the user to the actual number that the Library of Congress currently uses, or a note explaining Library of Congress practice.

Access to the online version of the full Library of Congress Classification is available on the World Wide Web by subscription to Classification Web. Details about ordering and pricing may be obtained from the Cataloging Distribution Service at

<http://www.loc.gov/cds/>

New or revised numbers and captions are added to the L.C. Classification schedules as a result of development proposals made by the cataloging staff of the Library of Congress and cooperating institutions. Upon approval of these proposals by the editorial meeting of the Policy and Standards Division, new classification records are created or existing records are revised in the master classification database. Lists of newly approved or revised classification numbers and captions are posted on the World Wide Web at

<http://www.loc.gov/aba/cataloging/classification/weeklylists/>

Jolande Goldberg, law classification specialist, created this schedule. She and Libby Dechman, senior cataloging policy specialist, are responsible for coordinating the overall intellectual and editorial content of class K and its various subclasses. Kent Griffiths and Ethel Tillman, assistant editors, are responsible for creating new classification records, maintaining the master database, and creating index terms for the captions.

Barbara B. Tillett, Chief
Policy and Standards Division

September 2011

OUTLINE

KZ1-6795	Law of nations
KZ2-5.5	Bibliography
KZ24-38	Societies, etc.
KZ27-37	National
KZ(60)-62.5	Intergovernmental congresses and conferences
KZ(63)-1152	Sources. Fontes juris gentium
KZ118-194	Treaties and other international agreements
KZ119-165	To 1920
KZ170-173	1920-
KZ176-182.5	Boundary treaties
KZ183-183.5	Treaties of arbitration, investigation, etc.
KZ184-194	Peace treaties
KZ199-218	Judicial decisions and arbitral awards
KZ221-1152	By region or country
KZ1165-1208	Trials
KZ1168-1208	Trials of international crimes
KZ1234-1236	Legal research. Legal bibliography
KZ1249-1252	International law and other disciplines
KZ1255-1273	Theory and principles
KZ1267-1273	Domain of the law of nations
KZ1284-1285.5	Methodology
KZ1287-1296	Codification of the law of nations
KZ1298-1304	The law of treaties. System of treaty law
KZ(1319)-(1327)	International legal regimes
KZ1329-3085	Early/Medieval development to ca. 1900. Ius Naturae et Gentium
KZ1330-1339	Peace of Westphalia to the French Revolution (1648-1789)
KZ1345-1369	French Revolution to the American Civil War (1789-1861)
KZ1373-1387.2	American Civil War to the First Conference of the Hague (1861-1899)
KZ2064-3085	Publicists. Writers on public international law
KZ3092-3405	20th century
KZ3110-3405	Publicists. Writers on public international law
KZ3410	21st century
KZ3670-3881	Objects of the law of nations. Territory and its different parts
KZ3900-(5490)	The international legal community and members
KZ3910-(5490)	Subjects of the law of nations
KZ4002-4080	The state
KZ4110	By region
KZ4112-4820	By state

OUTLINE

KZ1-7500	Law of nations
	The international legal community and members
	Subjects of the law of nations - Continued
KZ4850-(5490)	Intergovernmental ogranizations. IGOs
KZ4853-(4934)	The League of Nations
KZ(4935)-5275	The United Nations
KZ5330-(5490)	Regional organizations
KZ5510-6299	International law of peace and peace enforcement
KZ5586-5893	The system of collective security
KZ5615-5893	Arms control and disarmament regimes
KZ5637-5645	Conventional arms control
KZ5647-5686	Nuclear (Strategic) arms limitation
KZ5687-5788.5	Nuclear weapon free zones and zones of peace
KZ5834-5865	Other weapons of mass destruction
KZ5870-5893	Mutual and balanced reduction of armed forces
KZ5900-5967	Military pact systems for collective self-defense
KZ6009-6299	Pacific settlement of international disputes and conflict resolution
KZ6115-6299	Arbitration and adjudication
KZ6350-6785	Enforced settlement of international disputes
KZ6360-6373	Non-military coercion
KZ6374-(6377)	Threat of force
KZ6378-6785	Law of war and neutrality. Jus belli
KZ6427-6437	Warfare on land
KZ6440-6530	Humanitarian law
KZ6540-6660	Warfare on sea
KZ6665-6714	Air warfare
KZ6730-6795	The end of war. Armistice. Surrender. Postliminy
KZ7000-7500	International criminal law and procedure
KZ7011-7220	International criminal law
KZ7139-7220	International crimes or groups of crimes
KZ7140	Aggression. Crimes against peace
KZ7145-7177	Crimes against humanity. War crimes
KZ7180-7188	Genocide
KZ7198-7220	Other crimes under international law
KZ7230-7490	International criminal courts
KZ7250-7490	International Criminal Court (2002-)
KZ7495-7500	Victims of crimes

OUTLINE

KZA1002-(4205)	Law of the sea
KZA1040-1065	Intergovernmental congresses and conferences
KZA1118-1122	Treaties and other international agreements
KZA1340-1417	Concepts and principles
KZA1340	Mare clausum doctrine
KZA1348-1405	Mare liberum doctrine
KZA1430-1690	Maritime boundaries
KZA1630-1664	Continental shelf
KZA(3481)-(3900)	Marine resources conservation and development
KZA(3891)-(3900)	High-seas fisheries and fisheries regimes
KZA4130-(4205)	Public order of the oceans
KZD1002-6715	Space law. Law of outer space
KZD1040-1065	Intergovernmental congresses and conferences
KZD1118-1122	Treaties and other international agreements
KZD1340-1400	Concepts and principles. Theory
KZD1390-1400	Regulated use theory
KZD1410	The source of the law of space
KZD1420-1455	Boundaries
KZD3489-4406	Peaceful uses of outer space
KZD3489.5-3608	Space resources
KZD4030-4326	Public order in space and outer space
KZD4080-4210	Space flight
KZD(4301)-4310	Space communication
KZD4320.2-4326	Rescue operations in outer space
KZD4400-4406	Liability for accidents
KZD5614-6715	Un-peaceful uses of outer space
KZD5620-5622.2	Treaties and other international agreements
KZD5648-5680.2	Disarmament and demilitarization regimes in outer space

Law of nations

Class here works on legal principles recognized by nations, and rules governing conduct of nations and their relations with one another, including supra-regional Intergovernmental Organizations (IGO's) and the legal regimes governing such organizations

Class here the sources of international law, i.e. the law of treaties, arbitral awards and judicial decisions of the international courts

For organizations with missions limited to a particular region, see the appropriate K subclass for the regional organization (e. g. KJE for the Council of Europe)

For works on comparative and uniform law of two or more countries in different regions, and on private international law (Conflict of laws), see subclass K

Bibliography

For bibliography of special topics, see the topic

2 Bibliography of bibliography

3 General bibliography

4 Library catalogs. Union lists

5 Bibliography of periodicals, society publications, collections, etc.

For indexes to a particular publication, see the publication

5.5 Indexes to periodical articles

Periodicals

For periodical articles consisting primarily of informative material, e. g. news letters, bulletins, etc. relating to a particular subject, see the subject. For collected papers, proceedings, etc. of a particular congress, see the congress. For particular society publications, e. g. directories, see the society

For periodicals consisting predominantly of legal articles, regardless of subject matter and jurisdiction see K1+

21 Annuals. Yearbooks

Class here annual publications and surveys on current international law developments and analysis of recent events, including official document collections

e. g. Annuaire français de droit international; Asian Yearbook of International Law; British Yearbook of International Law; Jahrbuch für internationales Recht; Suid-Afrikaanse jaarboek vir volkereg

For annual reports on legal activities of intergovernmental organizations, see the organization (e. g. International Court of Justice Yearbook; Yearbook of the United Nations, etc.)

For subject oriented yearbooks, see the subject

For proceedings, reports, etc. of annual conferences and conventions of societies, see the convention

22 Monographic series

Societies. Associations. Academies, etc. for the study of international law and legal development
Class here works on individual learned societies and their activities
Including reports, bylaws, proceedings, directories, etc., and works about a society
For a society limited to a particular subject, see the subject
For substantive periodicals authored by such societies see K1+
For societies' annual surveys on international law development, etc. see KZ21

24.A-Z International, A-Z
24.H35 Hague. Academy of International Law. Académie de Droit International
24.I47 Institute of International Law. Institut de Droit International
24.I48 International Law Association
Previously Association for the Reform and Codification of the Law of Nations (1873-1895)

National
27.A-Z North American, A-Z
Including United States and Canada
27.A65 American Bar Association. Section of International and Comparative Law
27.A67 American Society of International Law
28.A-Z Central and South American, A-Z
European
31.A-Z English, A-Z
31.B75 British Institute of International and Comparative Law
32.A-Z French, A-Z
33.A-Z German, A-Z
33.D48 Deutsche Gesellschaft fuer Voelkerrecht
34.A-Z Italian, A-Z
35.A-Z Spanish and Portuguese, A-Z
35.2.A-Z Russian, A-Z
35.3.A-Z Other European, A-Z
Asian and Pacific
36.A-Z Australian, A-Z
36.2.A-Z Indian, A-Z
36.3.A-Z Japanese, A-Z
36.4.A-Z Other Asian and Pacific, A-Z
37.A-Z African and Middle Eastern, A-Z

Intergovernmental congresses and conferences. By name of the congress

Including ad hoc conferences of heads of state

For intergovernmental congresses on a particular subject, see the subject and/or period, e.g. the International Criminal Court, KZ7259

For The Hague International Peace Conference, 1899 see KZ6015+

For The Hague International Peace Conference, 1907 see KZ6020+

<60> Congress of Berlin, 1878
see KZ1383

<61> Berlin West Africa Conference, 1884-1885
see KZ1385

Geneva Conferences and Conventions
see the subject, e. g. Geneva Convention, July 6, 1906 (Relief of sick and wounded), KZ6464.2+

London International Naval Conference, 1908-1909 see KZ6545+

Brussels Conference, 1874 see KZ6381+

Congress of Vienna, 1814-1815 see KZ1355

Interparliamentary Union. Conference

62 Serials

62.2 Monographs. By date

62.5.A-Z Other, A-Z

Sources. Fontes juris gentium

<63> Basic documents for the study of international relations and diplomacy
see JZ63

Bibliography

Goergisch, Petrus, 1699-1746. Regesta chronologico diplomatica (1740-1744) see KZ625

General

64 Collective and selective

Class here general collections of treaties and other instruments of international law, and cases combined

Named collections

66 Dumont, Jean, baron de Carscroon, 1667-1727. Corpus universel diplomatique du droit des gens (1726-1731)

69 Martens, Karl, Freiherr von, 1790-1863. Receuil manuel et pratique de traités, conventions et autres actes diplomatiques, 1846-1857 (1885-1888)

Hörschelmann, Friedrich Ludwig Anton, Europäisches Staats-, Kriegs- und Friedenslexicon see KZ626

72 Strupp, Karl. Urkunden zur Geschichte des Völkerrechts (1911)

Sources. Fontes juris gentium
General
Named collections -- Continued
74 Wenck, Friedrich August Wilhelm, 1741-1810. Codex juris gentium (1781)
Treaties and other international agreements. Conventions
For boundary treaties see KZ176+
For peace treaties see KZ184+
For collections of treaties of a particular country with other countries see KZ235.3+
For works about treaties as a source of international law see KZ1298+
Comprehensive
118 Bibliography. Indexes. Registers. Digests. Repertories
e. g.
Bowman, M.J. Multilateral treaties; index and current status (1984)
Harvard index
Myers, Denys Peter. Manual of collections of treaties (1922)
Parry, Clive. Index-guide to treaties see KZ120
United States. Dept. of State. Catalogue of treaties (1919)
United States. Dept. of State. A tentative list of treaty collections (1919)
World Treaty Index see KZ173
By period
To 1920
For ancient law, see KL700+
For ius gentium (Rome), see KJA3320+
119 Bernard, Jacques, 1658-1718. Recueil des traitez de paix, de trêve, de neutralité ... de commerce ... (1700)
A general collections of treatys (1732-)
119.2 Gareis, Karl von. Vierzehn der wichtigsten voelkerrechtlichen Vertraege
120 Parry, Clive
e. g.
Consolidated Treaty series (1648 to ca. 1918/20, commencement of the League series)(1969-1981)
Index-guide to treaties: based on the consolidated treaty series (1979-1986)
133 Voss, Christian Daniel, 1761-1821. Geist der merkwürdigsten Bündnisse
133.2 Wenck, Friedrich August Wilhelm, 1741-1810. Codex juris gentium (1781-95)

Sources. Fontes juris gentium
Treaties and other international agreements. Conventions
By period
To 1920 -- Continued
Recueil. Recueil Général and Nouveau Recueil Général
Class here the compilations of treaties begun by Georg Friedrich von Martens and continued by his successors

142 Recueil des principaux traités (1791-1801). G.F. von Martens
142.2 Supplément au Recueil des principaux traités (1802-08). G.F. von Martens
142.3 Recueil des traités (1817-35). G.F. von Martens, K. von Martens
142.4 Nouveau Recueil de traités (1830-39). G.F. von Martens, K. von Martens, J.C.F. Saalfeld, F.W.A. Murhard
142.5 Nouveaux supplémens au Recueil de traités (1839-42). F.W.A. Murhard
142.52 Table général chronologique et alphabétique du Recueil des traités (1837-43)
142.6 Nouveau Recueil général de traités, conventions et autres transactions (1843-75). F.W.A. Murhard, J.K.A. Murhard, J. Pinhas, K.F.L. Samwer, Julius Hopf
142.7 Table général du Recueil des traités de G.F. Martens et de ses continuateurs. Julius Hopf
142.8 Nouveau Recueil général de traités et autres actes relatifs aux rapports de droit international (1876-1908). K.F.L. Samwer, J. Hopf, Felix Stoerk
142.9 Nouveau Recueil général de traités et autres actes relatifs aux rapports de droit international (1909-14). Heinrich Triepel
143 Carpentier, Adrien Louis. Recueil de traités, conventions et déclarations de droit international (1910)
151 Bridgman, Raymond Landon. The first book of world law (1972)
151.2 Hurst, Michael. Key treaties for the Great Powers 1814-1914
163 Stoecker, Helmuth. Handbuch der Verträge
164 Descamps, E.E.F., Baron, and Renault, J.L.
e. g.
Recueil international des traités du XIXe siècle (1914-)

Sources. Fontes juris gentium
Treaties and other international agreements. Conventions
By period
To 1920
Descamps, E.E.F., Baron, and Renault, J.L. -- Continued
Recueil international des traités du XXe siècle (1904-1921)
165 Other collections
1920-
Treaty series of intergovernmental organizations
League of Nations
170 Registration of treaties. Enregistrement des Traités
170.5 Treaty Series. Recueil des traités (L.N.T.S.) (1920-1945)
Including indexes that are part of the treaty series
United Nations
For treaties and agreements (individual or collected) establishing the UN, or supplementary and amendatory agreements see KZ4990.2
171 Indexes. Registers
e. g.
Signatures, ratifications ..., etc. concerning the multilateral conventions of which the Secretary-General acts as depository (1949-)
Multilateral treaties deposited with the Secretary-General
Statement of treaties and international agreements registered or filed and recorded with the Secretariat
Vambery, Joseph T. Cumulative list and index of treaties .. registered .. with the Secretariat of the UN (1977)
Cumulative index to the general international agreements of the UN treaty series (1984)
172 Treaty Series: treaties and international agreements registered or filed and recorded with the Secretariat of the United Nations. Recueil des traités (U.N.T.S.) (1946-)
172.8 Other collections
173 Indexes. Registers and other finding aids. By editor or compiler
e. g.
Grenville, J.A.S. The major international treaties, 1914-1945
The major international treaties, 1914-1973

Sources. Fontes juris gentium
Treaties and other international agreements. Conventions
Collections. Selections
1920-
Indexes. Registers and other finding aids. By editor or compiler
Grenville, J.A.S. The major international treaties, 1914-1945 -- Continued
The major international treaties since 1945 (J.A.S. Grenville, Bernard Wasserstein)
Rohn, Peter H. Treaty profiles (1976)
Rohn, Peter H. World treaty index (1974; 1983)
Boundary treaties
176 Indexes and tables. Registers. Regesta. Repertoria
176.2 Collections. Selections
North America
United States
177 Indexes and tables. Registers
177.2 Collections. Selections
177.3 Proposed treaties. Drafts
Including (contemporary) comments on the draft
177.5 Individual treaties. By date of signature
Subarrange each by Table K5
Canada
178 Indexes and tables. Registers
178.2 Collections. Selections
178.3 Proposed treaties. Drafts
Including (contemporary) comments on the draft
178.5 Individual treaties. By date of signature
Subarrange each by Table K5
Latin America
179 Indexes and tables. Registers
179.2 Collections. Selections
179.3 Proposed treaties. Drafts
Including (contemporary) comments on the draft
179.5.A-Z Individual treaties. By country, A-Z
Subarrange treaties of each country by date of signature. Further subarrange each treaty by Table K5
e.g.
179.5.H2 date Haiti
179.5.H2 1929 Le traité des frontieres, Haitano-Dominicaines, 1929 (Table K5)
Europe
180 Indexes and tables. Registers
180.2 Collections. Selections
180.3 Proposed treaties. Drafts
Including (contemporary) comments on the draft

Sources. Fontes juris gentium
Treaties and other international agreements. Conventions
Boundary treaties
Europe -- Continued
180.5.A-Z Individual treaties. By country, A-Z
Subarrange treaties of each country by date of signature. Further subarrange each treaty by Table K5
Asia and Pacific Regions
181 Indexes and tables. Registers
181.2 Collections. Selections
181.3 Proposed treaties. Drafts
Including (contemporary) comments on the draft
181.5.A-Z Individual treaties. By country, A-Z
Subarrange treaties of each country by date of signature. Further subarrange each treaty by Table K5
Africa. Middle East
182 Indexes and tables. Registers
182.2 Collections. Selections
182.3 Proposed treaties. Drafts
Including (contemporary) comments on the draft
182.5.A-Z Individual treaties. By country, A-Z
Subarrange treaties of each country by date of signature. Further subarrange each treaty by Table K5
Treaties of arbitration, investigation, mediation, conciliation, and compulsory adjudication
183 Indexes and tables. Registers. Regesta. Repertoria. Surveys and other finding aids
e. g. DeWolf, Francis C., General synopsis of treaties of arbitration (1933)
183.2 Collections. Selections
183.3 Proposed treaties. Drafts. Model treaties (Collected)
183.5.A-Z Individual treaties. By country, A-Z
Subarrange treaties of each country by date of signature. Further subarrange each treaty by Table K5
Peace treaties
Class here treaties settling a conflict or war, and treaties of peace efforts before or during the war
For treaties of "amity, alliance and commerce" see KZ221+
184 Indexes and tables. Registers. Regesta. Repertoires, etc.
e. g.
Ribier, Gabriel de, 1831-1892. Répertoire des traités de paix .. (1895-99)
Tétot, archiviste, 1810-1871. Répertoire traités de paix (1866-73)
Treaties and alliances of the world; an international survey (Keesing's contemporary archives)

Sources. Fontes juris gentium
Treaties and other international agreements. Conventions
Peace treaties -- Continued
184.2 Collections. Selections (Universal and regional). By editor or compiler
Including early collections (to 1914)
e. g.
Corpus pacificationum, 1792-1913 (1924)
Dumont, Jean, baron de Carlscroon (1667-1727)
Recueil des principaux traitez de paix .. (1698)
Recueil des principaux traitez de paix .. (1703)
Recueil des diverse traitez de paix, de confederation .. (1707) see KZ626
Nouveau recueil de traitez, d'alliance, commerce, de paix .. de l'Europe (1710) see KZ626
A general collection of treatys, declarations of war .. relating to peace and war among the Potentates of Europe from 1648 to the present .. (1710)
Garden, Guillome de. Histoire général des traités de paix .. (1848-87)
Israel, Fred L., Major peace treaties of modern history, 1648-1967 (1967-80)
Koch, Christoph Guillaume de, 1737-1813. Histoire .. des traités de paix .. (1817-1818)
Mas Latrie, Louis de, comte, 1815-1897. Traités de paix et de commerce .. (1865)
Recueil des traitez de paix, conclus depuis le commencement du Congrez d'Utrecht .. (1715)
Saint-Prest, Jean Yves de, d. 1720. Histoire des traités de paix (1725)
Schweitzer, Michael, Friedensvoelkerrecht (1979)
184.3 Proposed treaties. Drafts. Model treaties
For League of Nations. Model treaty to strengthen the means for preventing war see KZ6038
184.5 General works. Studies on treaties
By period
To ca. 1890 see KZ1327.6+
1890-1914
Collections see KZ184.2
184.6 Multilateral. By date of signature
184.7.A-Z Bilateral. By country, A-Z
Subarrange treaties of each country by date of signature. Further subarrange each treaty by Table K5
1914-1920. World War I to the Charter of the League of Nations
World War I

Sources. Fontes juris gentium
Treaties and other international agreements. Conventions
Peace treaties
By period
1914-1920. World War I to the Charter of the League of Nations
World War I -- Continued
Treaties of peace efforts during and towards the end of the war
185 Collections. Selections
185.2 Multilateral. By date of signature
185.5.A-Z Bilateral. By country, A-Z
Subarrange treaties of each country by date of signature. Further subarrange each treaty by Table K5
Peace treaties
Including all treaties and other international agreements on subsequent reparation (war debt) and territorial settlements
Including all treaties of the Allied and Associated Powers (1914-1920)
186 Collections. Selections
Including surrender documents
Multilateral
186.2 Treaty of Versailles, June 28, 1919 (Table K5)
186.22 Polish Minorities Treaty, July 28, 1919 (Table K5)
186.23 Treaty of St. Germain, September 10, 1919 (Table K5)
186.24 Treaty of Neuilly-sur-Seine, November 27, 1919 (Table K5)
186.25 Treaty of Trianon, June 4, 1920 (Table K5)
186.26 Treaty of Sèvres, August 10, 1920 (Table K5)
186.27 Treaty of Lausanne, July 24, 1923 (Table K5)
186.5.A-Z Bilateral. By country, A-Z
Subarrange treaties of each country by date of signature. Further subarrange each treaty by Table K5
1920 to the end of World War II (1945)
Particular conflicts or wars
World War II
Treaties of peace efforts during and towards the end of the war
188 Collections. Selections
188.2 Multilateral. By date of signature
Subarrange each by Table K5

Sources. Fontes juris gentium
Treaties and other international agreements. Conventions
Peace treaties
By period
1920 to the end of World War II (1945)
Particular conflicts or wars
World War II
Treaties of peace efforts during and towards the end of the war -- Continued

188.5.A-Z Bilateral. By country, A-Z
Subarrange treaties of each country by date of signature. Further subarrange each treaty by Table K5

188.6 Peace treaties. Treaties with Axis powers (Collections and selections)

Treaties and other agreements with regard to Germany
Including treaties on subsequent territorial settlements

189 Collections. Selections
Including surrender documents

189.2 Multilateral. By date of signature
Subarrange each by Table K5

189.5.A-Z Bilateral. By country, A-Z
Subarrange treaties of each country by date of signature. Further subarrange each treaty by Table K5

Treaties and other agreements with regard to Italy
Including treaties on subsequent territorial settlements

190 Collections. Selections
Including surrender documents

190.2 Multilateral. By date of signature
Subarrange each by Table K5

190.5.A-Z Bilateral. By country, A-Z
Subarrange treaties of each country by date of signature. Further subarrange each treaty by Table K5

Treaties and other agreements with regard to Japan

191 Collections. Selections
Including surrender documents

191.2 Multilateral. By date of signature
Subarrange each by Table K5

Sources. Fontes juris gentium
Treaties and other international agreements. Conventions
Peace treaties
By period
1920 to the end of World War II (1945)
Particular conflicts or wars
World War II
Treaties and other agreements with regard to Japan -- Continued

191.5.A-Z Bilateral. By country, A-Z
Subarrange treaties of each country by date of signature. Further subarrange each treaty by Table K5

192.A-Z Treaties and agreements with regard to other countries, A-Z
Under each:
.xA15-.xA199 Collections. Selections
.xA2 Multilateral treaties. By date of signature
.xA5-.xA599 Bilateral treaties. By country and date of signature

Other treaties and agreements
193 Collections. Selections
193.2 Multilateral. By date of signature (Table K5)
193.5.A-Z Bilateral. By country, A-Z
Subarrange treaties of each country by date of signature. Further subarrange each treaty by Table K5

1945-
194.A-Z Particular conflict or war. By name, A-Z
Under each:
.xA15-.xA199 Collections. Selections
.xA2 Multilateral treaties. By date of signature
.xA5-.xA599 Bilateral treaties. By country and date of signature

194.F35 Falkland Islands War, 1982
194.I54 India-Pakistan Conflict, 1971
194.I73 Iran-Iraq War, 1980-1988
194.I75 Iraq-Kuwait Crisis, 1990-1991
194.I77 Israel-Arab Wars, 1948-
For agreements between Israel and the Palestinian National Authority, see KMM707+
194.K67 Korean War, 1950-1953
194.V54 Vietnam War, 1961-1975

Judicial decisions and arbitral awards. Law reports
Including pleadings

Sources. Fontes juris gentium
Judicial decisions and arbitral awards. Law reports -- Continued
199 Universal collections
International arbitration. Cases and claims. Awards
200 General collections
For arbitration cases and claims (collected and individual), and awards by region or country see KZ221+
200.5 Indexes. Digests
Permanent Court of Arbitration. Cour permanente d'arbitrage (1900-)
201 Indexes
202 Digests. Summaries. Analytical abstracts. Repertory
Reports of international arbitral awards. Recueil
203 Serials
204 Monographs. By date
Permanent Court of International Justice. Cour permanente de justice. PCIJ (1920-1946)
Reports. Recueil
206 Indexes
207 Digests. Summary of judgments. Analytical abstracts. Repertory
General collections. Selections. With or without pleadings
208 Serials
209 Monographs. By date
210 Pleadings
International Court of Justice. Cour internationale de justice. ICJ (1946-)
Bibliography see KZ6272
Yearbooks. Annuaire see KZ6273
Annual report to the UN General Assembly
see JZ5010.2 Supplement No. 4
Reports. Recueil
Including judgments, advisory opinions, and orders
212 Indexes
213 Digests. Summary of judgments. Analytical abstracts. Advisory opinions. Orders. Repertory
General collections. Selections. With or without pleadings
214 Serials
215 Monographs. By date
Pleadings. Oral arguments. Documents
218 Collections
218.2 Individual documents

Sources. Fontes juris gentium
Judicial decisions and arbitral awards. Law reports -- Continued

(218.92-220.2) International Criminal Court. Cour pénale internationale. ICC (2002-)
see KZ7295+

By region or country
Countries that have been assigned a 10-number span are subarranged by Table K23 ; countries that have been assigned a 1-number span are subarranged by Table K24
Arbitration cases and claims are entered under defendant nation (e. g. KZ905.A84AK89 (Table K24), Kuwait claims vs. Iraq); group claims or cases are entered under name of nation from which claim derives its name

The Americas and West Indies

221-230 General (Table K23 modified)

(230.A-Z) This number not used

United States

Department of State documents and papers

231 General collections
Including Department of State Bulletin (previously Treaty Information bulletin); US Department of State Dispatch; Documents on American Foreign relations; International Organizations and Conference Series; etc.

Secretary of State

232 Reports
Including management reports, press releases, speeches, etc.

232.5 Diplomatic correspondence
Class here routine correspondence
Cf. Classes D - F for correspondence covering special events

Diplomatic correspondence and papers relating to the foreign relations of the US

233 Serials

233.5 Indexes. Lists of documents, etc. By date

233.6 Relations with particular countries. By country

234 President's messages related to treaties and other international agreements

United States Congress. Legislative documents
For the American State Papers see KF11
For committee hearings see KF24.8+
For House and Senate committee reports see KF29.7+

Senate. Committee on Foreign Relations
Cf. KF30.7+ Senate reports

Sources. Fontes juris gentium
By region or country
The Americas and West Indies
United States
United States Congress. Legislative documents
Senate. Committee on Foreign Relations -- Continued
234.2 Collections
234.3 Executive reports. By date
House. Committee on International Relations
Cf. KF31.7+ House reports
234.4 Collections
234.5 Particular. By date
Other documents and papers (administrative and executive)
see class J
Treaties and other international agreements.
Conventions
For US boundary, arbitration and peace treaties see KZ176+
235 Indexes. Digests and other aids
e. g. Index to International Treaties and Agreements (Erwin C. Surrency)
For U.S. Department of State. Treaty Information bulletin see KZ231+
Collections
Serials
Including official and non-official series
235.3 United States treaties and other International Agreements (UST)
235.32 Treaties And Other International Acts Series (Slip treaties; TIAS)
235.5 Consolidated treaties and international agreements. Current document service: United States (CTIA)
Monographs
Including official and private editions
236 By date
e. g. Treaties and other international agreements of the United States of America (Charles I. Bevans, 1968-1976); Treaties in Force (Bryan, Henry L., 1899)
236.3.A-Z By region or country, A-Z
237.2 Individual treaties. By date of signature
Indexes. Digests see KZ235

Sources. Fontes juris gentium
By region or country
The Americas and West Indies
United States
Treaties and other international agreements.
Conventions -- Continued
237.7 Cases. Decisions. Digests of decisions, opinions, etc.
Including United States attorneys general's opinions on international law questions
Cases, claims, etc.
Class here documents of, and works on, cases and claims before negotiated arbitration commissions or tribunals to which the United States or a United States citizen is a party, including historic cases. Cutter by name of case, claim, or defendant nation. For group claims, Cutter by name of case, claim, or plaintiff nation, e. g. .C5, Chilean claims; .S7, Spanish treaty claims
For reports of the Permanent Court of Arbitration see KZ201+
For reports of the International Courts of Justice see KZ206+
238.A2 General collections
Alabama claims
238.A4 Documents, correspondence, etc. prior to Treaty of Washington. By date
Treaty of Washington see KZ237.2
238.A42 The arbitration. Correspondence, etc.
The American case
Collections. General statement, and other documents
238.A43 American editions
238.A48 Foreign editions
Special documents
238.A5 1872 (dated)
Chronologically: American official edition; foreign editions, including translations
238.A51 1872 (undated)
238.A53 After 1872
The British case
238.A54 Collections (English editions)
238.A58 Collections (Foreign editions)
Special documents
238.A6 1872 (dated)
238.A61 1872 (undated)
238.A63 After 1872
The Tribunal

Sources. Fontes juris gentium
By region or country
The Americas and West Indies
United States
Cases, claims, etc.
Alabama claims
The arbitration. Correspondence, etc.
The Tribunal -- Continued

238.A64 Collections
238.A65 Documents prior to the award
238.A66 Decision and award
238.A67 Other
238.A687 United States Court of Commissioners, 1874
United States Court of Commissioners, 1882
238.A69 Proceedings
238.A692 Rules, opinions, etc., 1882-1885
238.A695 Separate documents. By date
238.A7 Semiofficial and nonofficial. By date
238.A8-.A85 Mixed Commission on British and American claims under Article XII of the Treaty of Washington, 1871
238.A8 British claims
Including memorials, briefs, decisions, testimony
238.A81 American claims
Including memorials, briefs, decisions, testimony
238.A83 List of claims
238.A85 Other documents, and nonofficial matter. By date
238.A95 Tripartite Claims Commission 1925 (US vs. Austria, Hungary)
238.B83 American claims against Bulgaria
238.C5 Chilean claims. Chilean Claims Commission
238.F6 French and American claims
Claims originating 1860-1871 (Mexican intervention 1860-1866, Franco-German War 1870-1871); French and American Claims Commission, 1880-1884
French Spoliation claims
Including spoliations prior to July, 1801 (treaties and awards, etc. under conventions of 1803; 1831; treaty with Spain, 1819; etc.)
238.F72 General collections
United States
238.F73 Documents. By date
238.F74A-.F74Z Particular claims. By name, A-Z
238.F743 French documents
238.F75 Nonofficial documents (pamphlets, etc.). By date
238.F77A-.F77Z Other special, A-Z

Sources. Fontes juris gentium
By region or country
The Americas and West Indies
United States
Cases, claims, etc. -- Continued

238.F8 Fur seal arbitration. Bering Sea Claims Commission
238.G3 Mixed Claims Commission (United States and Germany) 1922-1940
Including rules, commissioners' reports, decisions, etc.
238.G7 Hawaiian claims Gt. Britain vs. United States
238.I7 United States vs. Iran (Iranian United States Tribunal decisions)
238.N6 Northeastern fisheries
238.P5 Pious Fund cases
238.S7 Spanish claims. Spanish Treaty Claims Commission
239 Cases and claims. By date
Including private claims
245.A-.W American States, A-W
e. g.
245.T4 Texas Republic
Confederate States diplomatic documents, etc. see JK9663+
351-360 Canada (Table K23)
360.5 Greenland (Table K24)
361-370 Mexico (Table K23)
Central America
371-380 General (Table K23 modified)
(380.A-Z) This number not used
381-390 Belize (Table K23)
391-400 Costa Rica (Table K23)
401-410 Guatemala (Table K23)
411-420 Honduras (Table K23)
421-430 Nicaragua (Table K23)
431-440 Panama (Table K23)
441-450 El Salvador (Table K23)
West Indies. Caribbean Area
Including Federation of the West Indies, 1958-1962
450.5 General works
451-460 Cuba (Table K23)
461-470 Haiti (Table K23)
471-480 Dominican Republic (Table K23)
483 Puerto Rico (Table K24)
484 Virgin Islands of the United States. Danish West Indies (Table K24)
485 British West Indies (Table K24)
<491> Danish West Indies
see KZ484

Sources. Fontes juris gentium
By region or country
The Americas and West Indies
West Indies. Caribbean Area -- Continued

493	Netherlands Antilles. Dutch West Indies (Table K24)
	Including Curaçao
	For Suriname (Dutch Guiana) see KZ574
495	French West Indies (Table K24)
	Including Guadeloupe and Martinique
	For French Guiana see KZ577
	South America
501-510	General (Table K23 modified)
(510.A-Z)	This number not used
511-520	Argentina (Table K23)
521-530	Bolivia (Table K23)
531-540	Brazil (Table K23)
541-550	Chile (Table K23)
551-560	Colombia (Table K23)
561-570	Ecuador (Table K23)
	Guiana
571	General works
	British Guiana. Guyana see KZ485
574	Suriname. Dutch Guiana (Table K24)
577	French Guiana (Table K24)
581-590	Paraguay (Table K23)
591-600	Peru (Table K23)
601-610	Uruguay (Table K23)
611-620	Venezuela (Table K23)
620.5	Falkland Islands (Table K24)
	Europe
621-630	General (Table K23 modified)
	Treaties and other international agreements. Conventions
625	Indexes. Registers. Digests. Repertoires
	e.g. Georgisch, Peter 1699-1746. Regesta chronologico-diplomatica, 1740-1744
	Collections
625.3	Serials
626	Monographs. By date
	e.g.
	Recueil des tous les traites modernes conclus entre les potentats d'Europe ... (1683)
	Bernard, Jacques, 1658-1718. Recueil des traitez de paix .. de l'Europe .. 1700 see KZ119

Sources. Fontes juris gentium
By region or country
Europe
General
Treaties and other international agreements. Conventions
Collections
Monographs. By date -- Continued
Dumont, Jean, d. 1726. Recueil de diverse traitéz .. (1707)
Recueil des diverse traitez de paix, de confederation .. (1707); Nouveau recueil de traitez, d'alliance, commerce, de paix .. de l'Europe (1710)
A general collection of treatys, declarations of war .. relating to peace and war among the Potentates of Europe from 1648 to the present .. (1710) see KZ184.2
Rousset de Missy, Jean, 1686-1762. Recueil historique d'actes .. et traitez (1728-1755)
Supplement au recueil des principaux traites de Dumont et Rousset (1807)
La Mallardière, Charles François Lefèvre de, d. 1804. Abregé des principaux traités .. (1778)
Saint-Prest, Jean Yves de, d. 1720. Histoire des traités see KZ183.2
Hoerschelmann, Friedrich Ludewig Anton, b. 1740. Europäisches staats-, kriegs- und friedenslexicon .. (1765-1766)
Oakes, Augustus, Sir, The Great European Treaties of the 19th Century (1918)
(630.A-Z) This number not used
Great Britain
631-640 General (Table K23 modified)
Class here works on England, and on England, Wales, Scotland and Northern Ireland combined
(640.A-Z) This number not used
641 Wales (Table K24)
642 Scotland (Table K24)
Gibraltar see KZ1046
643 Northern Ireland (Table K24)
645 Ireland. Eire (Table K24)
651-660 Austria. Austro-Hungarian Monarchy (Table K23)
661-670 Hungary (Table K23)
671-680 Czechoslovakia (to 1993). Czech Republic (Table K23)
680.5 Slovakia (1993-) (Table K24)
681-690 France (Table K23)

Sources. Fontes juris gentium
By region or country
Europe -- Continued
690.5 Monaco (Table K24)
Germany
Including the Federal Republic of Germany (to1992)
691-700 General (Table K23 modified)
700.A-Z Individual states, A-Z
700.B34 Baden
700.B38 Bavaria
700.G48 Germany, Democratic Republic (1949-1992)
700.P78 Prussia (Duchy)
700.W82 Wuerttemberg
701-710 Greece (Table K23)
Italy
711-720 General (Table K23 modified)
720.A-Z Individual states, A-Z
720.V45 Venice
722 Andorra (Table K24)
723 San Marino (Table K24)
724 Malta (Table K24)
The Benelux countries. Low countries
Holland see KZ741+
731-740 Belgium (Table K23)
The Netherlands. Holland
741-750 General (Table K23 modified)
750.A-Z Individual provinces, A-Z
Including historic (defunct) jurisdictions
750.5 Luxembourg (Table K24)
Russia. Soviet Union (to 1991)
751-760 General (Table K23 modified)
Including works on, and proceedings of, the Commonwealth of Independent States; of former Soviet Republics (collectively); and of other historic (defunct) states, etc.
760.A-Z Individual states, republics, etc., A-Z
Byelorussian SSR see KZ760.4
Estonia see KZ760.9
Finland see KZ760.8
Latvia see KZ760.92
Lithuania see KZ760.93
Poland see KZ760.7
White Russia see KZ760.4
760.2 Russia (Federation) (Table K24)
Caucasus
Armenia (Republic) see KZ923
Azerbaijan see KZ924

Sources. Fontes juris gentium
By region or country
Europe
Caucasus -- Continued
Georgia (Republic) see KZ925
760.4 Belarus (Table K24)
760.5 Moldova (Table K24)
760.6 Ukraine (Table K24)
760.7 Poland (Table K24)
760.8 Finland (Table K24)
Baltic countries
760.9 Estonia (Table K24)
760.92 Latvia (Table K24)
760.93 Lithuania (Table K24)
Scandinavia
761-770 General (Table K23 modified)
(770.A-Z) This number not used
771-780 Denmark (Table K23)
For Greenland see KZ360.5
781-790 Iceland (Table K23)
791-800 Norway (Table K23)
801-810 Sweden (Table K23)
Spain
811-820 General (Table K23 modified)
820.A-Z Individual states, provinces, regions, etc., A-Z
820.A7 Aragon
Gibraltar see KZ1046
821-830 Portugal (Table K23)
831-840 Switzerland (Table K23)
840.5 Liechtenstein (Table K24)
Southeastern Europe. Balkan States
840.9 General (Table K24)
Greece see KZ701+
841-850 Turkey (Table K23)
850.3 Cyprus (Table K24)
850.5 Albania (Table K24)
851-860 Bulgaria (Table K23)
861-870 Montenegro (Table K23)
Romania
871-880 General (Table K23 modified)
880.A-Z Individual states, provinces, etc., A-Z
880.W35 Wallachia
881-890 Yugoslavia (to 1992). Serbia (Table K23)
893 Croatia (Table K24)
894 Bosnia and Hercegovina (Table K24)
896 Slovenia (Table K24)
897 Macedonia (Republic) (Table K24)

Sources. Fontes juris gentium
By region or country -- Continued
Asia
Middle East. Southwest Asia
898 General (Table K24)
900 Armenia (to 1921) (Table K24)
901 Bahrain (Table K24)
Gaza see KZ906
904 Iran (Table K24)
905 Iraq (Table K24)
906 Israel. Palestine (Table K24)
907 Jerusalem (Table K24)
908 Jordan (Table K24)
West Bank (Territory under Israeli occupation, 1967-) see KZ906
910 Kuwait (Table K24)
911 Lebanon (Table K24)
912 Oman (Table K24)
913 Palestine (to 1948) (Table K24)
914 Qatar (Table K24)
915 Saudi Arabia (Table K24)
Southern Yemen see KZ919
916 Syria (Table K24)
917 United Arab Emirates (Table K24)
918 Yemen (Table K24)
919 Yemen (People's Democratic Republic) (to 1990) (Table K24)
Caucasus
923 Armenia (Republic) (Table K24)
924 Azerbaijan (Table K24)
925 Georgia (Republic) (Table K24)
Turkey see KZ841+
Cyprus see KZ850.3
Central Asia
930 Kazakhstan (Table K24)
931 Kyrgyzstan (Table K24)
932 Tadjikistan (Table K24)
933 Turkmenistan (Table K24)
934 Uzbekistan (Table K24)
South Asia. Southeast Asia. East Asia
934.5 General (Table K24)
For works on both Asia and Pacific areas see KZ1105
935 Afghanistan (Table K24)
936 Bangladesh (Table K24)
937 Bhutan (Table K24)
938 Brunei (Table K24)

Sources. Fontes juris gentium
By region or country
Asia
South Asia. Southeast Asia. East Asia -- Continued
939 Burma. Myanmar (Table K24)
939.5 Cambodia (Table K24)
China (to 1949)
941-950 General (Table K23 modified)
950.A-Z Provinces, A-Z
950.A63 An-tung sheng
950.C53 Ch'a-ha-erh sheng
Fukien Province. Fuijan Sheng see KZ961+
950.H64 Ho-Chiang sheng
950.H75 Hsi-k'ang sheng
950.H76 Hsing-an sheng
950.J44 Je-ho sheng
Kwangsi Province. Kuang-hsi see KZ961+
Kwangtung Province. Guangdong Sheng see KZ961+
950.L53 Liao-pei sheng
950.N46 Neng-Chiang sheng
950.N56 Ning-hsia sheng
950.P56 Pin-Chiang sheng
Sikang Province see KZ961+
950.S85 Sui-yuan sheng
950.S87 Sung-Chiang sheng
950.T35 T'ai-wan sheng
951-960 China (Republic, 1949-). Taiwan (Table K23)
China (Peoples Republic, 1949-)
961-970 General (Table K23 modified)
970.A-Z Provinces, automonous regions and municipalities, A-Z
970.H66 Hong Kong
India
971-980 General (Table K23 modified)
980.A-Z States, Union Territories, etc., A-Z
Including historic (defunct) jurisdictions (e. g. princely states, presidencies, etc.)
980.A64 Andaman and Nicobar Islands
980.A65 Andrah Pradesh
980.A78 Arunchal Pradesh
980.A88 Assam
980.B55 Bihar
980.C35 Calcutta/Bengal Presidency
980.C53 Chandighar
980.D34 Dadra and Nagar Haveli
980.D45 Delhi

Sources. Fontes juris gentium
By region or country
Asia
South Asia. Southeast Asia. East Asia
India
General
States, Union Territories, etc. -- Continued

980.G63 Goa, Daman, and Diu
980.G85 Gujarat
980.H37 Haryana
980.H56 Himachal Pradesh
980.H84 Hyderabad
980.J35 Jaipur
980.J36 Jammu and Kashmir
980.K37 Karnataka
980.K47 Kerala
980.K85 Kumaon
980.L35 Lakshadweep
980.M34 Madhya Pradesh
980.M35 Madras Presidency
980.M36 Maharashtra
980.M37 Manipur
980.M45 Meghalaya
980.M59 Mizoram
Mysore see KZ980.U77
980.N35 Nagaland
980.O75 Orissa
980.P66 Pondicherry
980.P85 Punjab
980.R35 Rajasthan
980.S55 Sikkim
980.T35 Tamil Nadu
980.T75 Tripura
980.U77 Uttar Pradesh
980.W47 West Bengal
980.3 French Indochina (Table K24)
980.6 Indonesia (Table K24)
981-990 Japan (Table K23)
991 Korea (South) (Table K24)
992 Democratic People's Republic of Korea. Korea (North) (Table K24)
992.3 Korea (to 1945) (Table K24)
993 Laos (Table K24)
994 Macau (Table K24)
Malaysia
995 General (Table K24)
Individual states

Sources. Fontes juris gentium
By region or country
Asia
South Asia. Southeast Asia. East Asia
Malaysia
Individual states -- Continued

995.3 Straits Settlements (to 1942) (Table K24)
995.5 Federated Malay States (1896-1942) (Table K24)
995.7 Malayan Union (1946-1947) (Table K24)
995.8 Malaya (1948-1962) (Table K24)
996.A-Z States of East and West Malaysia (1957-), A-Z
996.F44 Federal Territory (Kuala Lumpur)
996.J65 Johor
996.K44 Kedah
996.K46 Kelantan
996.L33 Labuan
996.M35 Malacca
996.N45 Negri Sembilan
996.P35 Pahang
996.P47 Perak
996.P48 Perlis
996.P56 Pinang
996.S33 Sabah
Previously North Borneo
996.S37 Sarawak
996.S45 Selangor
996.T47 Terengganu
997 Maldives (Table K24)
998 Mongolia (Table K24)
Myanmar see KZ939
999 Nepal (Table K24)
1000 Pakistan (Table K24)
1001-1010 Philippines (Table K23)
1011 Singapore (Table K24)
1012 Sri Lanka. Ceylon (Table K24)
1013 Thailand (Table K24)
1014 Vietnam (1976-) (Table K24)
Including the periods up through 1945
1016 Vietnam (Republic). South Vietnam (1946-1975) (Table K24)
1017 Vietnam (Democratic Republic). North Vietnam (1946-1975) (Table K24)
Africa
1019 General (Table K24)
1020 Algeria (Table K24)
1021 Angola. Portuguese West Africa (Table K24)
1022 Benin. Dahomy. French West Africa (Table K24)

Sources. Fontes juris gentium
By region or country
Africa -- Continued

1023 Botswana. Bechuanaland Protectorate (Table K24)
1024 British Central Africa Protectorate (Table K24)
1025 British Indian Ocean Territory (Table K24)
1026 British Somaliland (Table K24)
1027 Burkina Faso. Upper Volta (Table K24)
1028 Burundi. Ruanda-Urandi (Table K24)
1029 Cameroon. French Trusteeship of Cameroun. British Southern Cameroons (Table K24)
1030 Cape Verde (Table K24)
1031 Central African Republic. Central African Empire (Ubangi Shari) (Table K24)
1032 Chad (Table K24)
1033 Comoros (Table K24)
1034 Congo (Brazzaville). Moyen-Congo (Table KZ2)
1035 Côte d'Ivoire. Ivory Coast (Table K24)
1036 Djibouti. French Somaliland. Afars and Issas (Table K24)
1037 East Africa Protectorate (Table K24)
1038 Egypt. United Arab Republic (Table K24)
1038.5 Eritrea (Table K24)
1039 Ethiopia. Abyssinia (Table K24)
1040 French Equatorial Africa (Table K24)
1041 French West Africa (Table K24)
1042 Gabon (Table K24)
1043 Gambia (Table K24)
1044 German East Africa (Table K24)
1045 Ghana. Gold Coast (Table K24)
1046 Gibraltar (Table K24)
1047 Guinea. French Guinea (Table K24)
1048 Guinea-Bissau. Portuguese Guinea (Table K24)
1049 Equatorial Guinea. Spanish Guinea (Table K24)
1050 Ifni (Table K24)
1051 Italian East Africa (Table K24)
1052 Italian Somaliland (Table K24)
1053 Kenya (Table K24)
1054 Lesotho. Basutholand (Table K24)
1055 Liberia (Table K24)
1056 Libya (Table K24)
1057 Madagascar. Malagasy Republic (Table K24)
1058 Malawi. Nyasaland (Table K24)
1059 Mali (Table K24)
1060 Mauritania (Table K24)
1061 Mauritius (Table K24)
1062 Mayotte (Table K24)
1063 Morocco (Table K24)

Sources. Fontes juris gentium
By region or country
Africa -- Continued

1064 Mozambique. Portuguese East Africa (Table K24)
1065 Namibia. German South-West Africa. South-West Africa (Table K24)
1066 Niger (Table K24)
1067 Nigeria. Colony and Protectorate of Nigeria (Table K24)
1068 Réunion (Table K24)
1069 Rwanda. Ruanda-Urundi (Table K24)
1070 Saint Helena (Table K24)
1071 Sao Tome and Principe (Table K24)
1072 Senegal (Table K24)
1073 Seychelles (Table K24)
1074 Sierra Leone (Table K24)
1075 Somalia. Somali Republic (Table K24)
South Africa, Republic of
1081-1090 General (Table K23 modified)
1090.A-Z Provinces and self-governing territories, etc., A-Z
Including former independent homelands
1090.B66 Bophuthatswana
1090.C36 Cape of Good Hope. Kaapland
1090.C57 Ciskei
1090.E36 Eastern Cape
Eastern Transvaal see KZ1090.M68
1090.F74 Free State. Orange Free State
1090.G38 Gauteng
1090.K93 KwaZulu-Natal. Natal
Including former KwaZulu Homeland areas
1090.M68 Mpulamanga. Eastern Transvaal
Natal see KZ1090.K93
1090.N64 North West
1090.N65 Northern Cape
1090.N66 Northern Province. Northern Transvaal
Northern Transvaal see KZ1090.N66
Orange Free State. Oranje Vrystaat see KZ1090.F74
1090.T73 Transkei
1090.T74 Transvaal
1090.V46 Venda
1090.W48 Western Cape
1091 Spanish West Africa (to 1958) (Table K24)
1092 Spanish Sahara (to 1975) (Table K24)
1093 Sudan (Table K24)
1094 Swaziland (Table K24)
1095 Tanzania. Tanganyika (Table K24)
1096 Togo. Togoland (Table K24)

Sources. Fontes juris gentium
By region or country
Africa -- Continued

1097 Tunisia (Table K24)
1098 Uganda. Protectorate of Uganda (Table K24)
1099 Congo (Democratic Republic). Zaire. Congo Free State (Belgian Congo) (Table K24)
1100 Zambia. Northern Rhodesia (Table K24)
1101 Zanzibar (to 1964) (Table K24)
1103 Zimbabwe. Southern Rhodesia (Table K24)

Pacific Area

1105 General (Table K24)
Including works on both Pacific and Asian areas

Australia

1111-1120 General (Table K23 modified)
1120.A-Z States and territories, A-Z
Including external territories
Australian Antarctic Territory see KWX125
1120.A88 Australian Capital Territory
1120.N48 New South Wales
1120.N67 Norfolk Island (External territory)
1120.N673 Northern Territory
1120.Q84 Queensland
1120.S68 South Australia
1120.T38 Tasmania
1120.V53 Victoria
1120.W48 Western Australia

New Zealand

1121 General (Table K24)
1122.A-Z Regions and overseas territories, A-Z
Ross Dependancy see KWX185

Other Pacific Area jurisdictions

1125 American Samoa (Table K24)
1126 British New Guinea (Territory of Papua) (Table K24)
1127 Cook Islands (Table K24)
1128 Easter Island (Table K24)
1129 Fiji (Table K24)
1130 French Polynesia (Table K24)
1131 German New Guinea (to 1914) (Table K24)
1132 Guam (Table K24)
1133 Kiribati (Table K24)
1134 Marshall Islands (Table K24)
1135 Micronesia (Federated States) (Table K24)
1136 Midway Islands (Table K24)
1137 Nauru (Table K24)
1138 Netherlands New Guinea (to 1963) (Table K24)
1139 New Caledonia (Table K24)

Sources. Fontes juris gentium
By region or country
Pacific Area
Other Pacific Area jurisdictions -- Continued
1140 Niue (Table K24)
1141 Northern Mariana Islands (Table K24)
1142 Pacific Islands (Trust Territory) (Table K24)
1143 Palau (Table K24)
1144 Papua New Guinea (Table K24)
1145 Pitcairn Island (Table K24)
1146 Solomon Islands (Table K24)
1147 Tonga (Table K24)
1148 Tuvalu (Table K24)
1149 Vanuatu (Table K24)
1150 Wake Islands (Table K24)
1151 Wallis and Futuna Islands (Table K24)
1152 Samoa. Western Samoa (Table KZ2)
Antarctica
see subclass KWX
1160 Encyclopedias
1161 Dictionaries. Terms and phrases. Vocabularies
1162 Legal maxims. Quotations
1163 Directories
Trials
1165 Boundary cases and trials
Class here boundary trials before the International Court of Justice
For boundary arbitration before an arbitral tribunal between two or more countries in a region see KZ238+
Trials of international crimes
Class here trials by international courts and ad hoc tribunals
Including war crime trials and other violations of humanitarian law (Geneva law)
For war crime trials, and trials of other international crimes by national courts, see the appropriate jurisdiction in K subclasses, e. g. Eichman trial, KMK44.E44
For collections of such trials by national courts in the same region, see the region
For trials before the International Criminal Court (ICC) see KZ1215+
Cf. KZ7139+ International crimes
1168 Bibliography
1168.5 General collections
Including comparative discussion of trials
By period
Early to end of World War I, 1918

Trials
Trials of international crimes
By period
Early to end of World War I, 1918 -- Continued
Bibliography see KZ1168
1169 Collections. Selections
Particular wars or international armed conflicts
World War I, 1914-1918
1170 General (Collected)
1170.5.A-Z Individual trials. By first named defendant or best known (popular) name, A-Z
Subarrange each by Table K2
1171.A-Z Trials during or after other wars or international armed conflicts. By name of war or conflict, A-Z
Subarrange each by Table KZ11
End of World War I to 1949
Bibliography see KZ1168
1173 Collections. Selections
Particular wars or international armed conflicts
World War II
Bibliography see KZ1168
1174 Collections. Selections
1174.5 General works
Nuremberg Trial of Major German War Criminals before the International Military Tribunal (IMT), 1945-1946
1175 Bibliography
1176 Collections. Selections
1176.5 General works
For general works about subsequent and individual trials, see KZ1177.A+ and KZ1179.A+
1177.A-Z Individual trials. By first named defendant or best known (popular) name, A-Z
Subarrange each by Table K2
1177.S77 Streicher, Julius, 1885-1946 (Table K2)
Subsequent proceedings, 1945-1949
Including trials in particular Zones of Allied Occupation, 1945-1955
For trials of German war criminals by German courts see KK73+
1178 General (Collected)
1179.A-Z Individual trials. By first named defendant or best known (popular) name, A-Z
Subarrange each by Table K2
1179.B45 Belsen Trial, 1945 (Table K2)
Eichmann, Adolph, 1906-1962
see KMK

Trials
Trials of international crimes
By period
End of World War I to 1949
Particular wars or international armed conflicts
World War II
Nuremberg Trial of Major German War Criminals before the International Military Tribunal (IMT), 1945-1946
Subsequent proceedings, 1945-1949
Individual trials. By first named defendant or best known (popular) name, A-Z -- Continued
1179.E36 Einsatzgruppen Trial, 1947-1948 (Table K2)
1179.H54 High Command Trial, 1948-1949 (Table K2)
1179.I23 I.G. Farben Trial, 1947-1948 (Table K2)
1179.J89 Justice case, 1947 (Table K2)
1179.M43 Medical Trial, 1946-1947 (Table K2)
1179.M56 Ministries Trial, 1948-1949 (Table K2)
1179.N38 Natzweiler Trial, 1946 (Table K2)
The Tokyo Judgment: International Military Tribunal for the Far East (IMTFE), 1946-1948
1180 Bibliography
1181 General (Collected)
1182.A-Z Individual trials. By first named defendant or best known (popular) name, A-Z
1182.A73 Araki, Sadao, 1877-1966 (Table K2)
1182.3 Yokohama Trials, 1945-1949
The Manila War Crime Trial, 1946
1183 General (Collected)
1184.A-Z Individual trials. By first named defendant or best known (popular) name, A-Z
1184.H66 Homma, Massaharu, 1887-1946 (Table K2)
1184.Y36 Yamashita, Tomoyuki, 1885-1946 (Table K2)
Class B and Class C War Crime Trials, 1946-1952
Class here trials of Class B and C war crimes held throughout Asia by military tribunals of United States, United Kingdom, China, Russia, Australia, New Zealand, Canada, France, Netherlands and Philippines
1185 General (Collective)
1186.A-Z Individual trials. By first named defendant or best known (popular) name, A-Z (Table K2)
1187.A-Z Trials during or after other wars or international armed conflicts. By name of war or conflict, A-Z
Subarrange each by Table KZ11
1949-

Trials
Trials of international crimes
By period
1949- -- Continued
Bibliography see KZ1168
1190 Collections. Selections
Particular wars or international armed conflicts
Cf. KZ6795.A+ Particular wars or conflicts
1191 Falkland Islands War, 1982 (Table KZ10)
1193 Iran-Iraq War, 1980-1988 (Table KZ10)
1195 India-Pakistan Conflict, 1971 (Table KZ10)
1197 Iraq-Kuwait Crisis, 1990-1991 (Table KZ10)
1199 Korean War, 1950-1953 (Table KZ10)
1201 Rwanda Civil War, 1994 (Table KZ10)
1203 Yugoslav War, 1991- (Table KZ10)
1208.A-Z Trials during or after other wars or international armed conflicts. By name of war or conflict, A-Z
Subarrange each by Table KZ11
1208.C36 Cambodian Civil War, 1970-1975 (Table KZ11)
1208.C45 Chadian Civil War, 1965- (Table KZ11)
1208.S53 Sierra Leone Civil War, 1991-2002 (Table KZ11)
1208.U33 Ugandan Insurgency, 1987- (Table KZ11)
Trials before the International Criminal Court (ICC)
1215 General (Collective)
1216.A-Z Individual trials. By first named defendant or best known name, A-Z
Legal research. Legal bibliography
Including methods of bibliographic research and how to find the law
1234 General works
1235 Electronic data processing
1236 Legal abbreviations. System of citation
Surveys of legal activities
Yearbooks containing such surveys, e. g. status reports concerning unification, approximation, cooperation, etc. see KZ21
Society publications containing such surveys see KZ24+
Legal education. Study and teaching
1237 General works
1238.A-Z By region or country, A-Z
Associations. Societies. Academies, etc.
General see KZ24+
International Bar Association see K109+
International Criminal Bar see KZ7045
1240 Conferences. Symposia
Intergovernmental congresses and conferences see KZ62+

1242 History
Class here comprehensive histories as well as histories of specific periods of international law
1242.5 Casebooks
For casebooks on particular subjects, see the subject
1243.A-Z Manuals and other works for particular groups of users, A-Z
International law and other disciplines or subjects
1249 Relation to social (behavioral) sciences
International law and religious legal systems see KB259+
1250 International law and political ideology. International socialist law
1251 Sociology of international law
1252 Relation to economics
Theory and principles
Class here works on the philosophy and doctrine of the Law of Nations
For the history of international relations, including the history of political doctrine and diplomacy see JZ1305+
For the history of international law see KZ1242
General works see KZ2064+
The concept of law
Ethics. Morality of law
1256 International public order. Ordre public
1257 Abuse of rights. Internationally wrongful acts
1258 Equity. Ex aequo et bono
Effectiveness, validity, enforceability of the law of nations
Cf. KZ6376 Enforced measures under UN Charter
1259 General works
1260 Certainty of law. Legal uncertainty
1261 Jus cogens
1262.A-Z Other topics, A-Z
1262.C65 Consent
1262.E849 Estoppel
1262.G64 Good faith
International public law and municipal law
Including Dualist view and Monistic doctrine
1263 Precedence of international public law
Implementation of Law of Nations by members of the international legal community
see class K subclasses
1265 Conflict between municipal and international public law
Domain of the Law of Nations
1267 General works
Globalization of law. Pluralistic law
1268 General works
1269 De-colonization and national self-determination

Theory and principles
Domain of the Law of Nations
Globalization of law. Pluralistic law -- Continued
The international society. Cooperative multilateralism
Class here works on the concept of interstate cooperation without central governing power
1270 General works
International cooperation through legal regimes see KZ1321
Rules of conduct in the international community
1272 General works
Enforcability of rules of conduct. Jus cogens see KZ1261
1273 Regionalism. Regional law. Supra-national law
For the law of particular regions, see the regional classification schedules, e. g. KJ-KJE for the regional European law
For sovereignty questions see KZ4041+
1275 Rule of law
The source of international law
1276 Religious principles, doctrines, and ideologies
1277 Custom. State practice. Consuetudo and opinio juris. Customary international law
1278 Official acts. Intergovernmental transactions
For treaty collections see KZ118+
For the system of treaty law see KZ1298+
1279 General principles. Principés généraux
Including doctrine and advisory opinion
1280 Decisions of tribunals and courts. Judicial precedent. Arbitral awards and rulings
Codes see KZ1289+
International legal regimes see KZ1322+
The UN system as source of international law see KZ4992.7+
Methodology
1284 General works
e. g. Albert Bleckmann, Methodenlehre des Völkerrechts; Albert Bleckmann, Funktionen der Lehre im Völkerrecht
1285 Legal hermeneutics. Interpretation and construction
Including interpretation of international public law and supranational law. Lacunae in international law
1285.5 Legal semantics. Terminology
Codification of the law of nations. International law making
Class here works on the precise formulation and systematization of customary international law present in state practice, precedent and doctrine
1287.A-Z Conferences. Commissions. Institutes, A-Z

Codification of the law of nations. International law making Conferences. Commissions. Institutes, A-Z -- Continued

1287.C6 Hague Conferences for the Codification of International Law, 1930

1287.I46 Institute for International Law

1287.I47 Interamerican Council of Jurists

1287.I57 International Commission of American Jurists

1287.I59 International Law Commission (United Nations)

Codes

1289 Official. Codification juridique

Class here documents issued by official bodies, e. g. League of Nations, UN International Law Commission, Panamerican Union, etc.

Including preparation of draft conventions on subjects not yet regulated by international law or not yet in practice by states (lacunae in customary law)

1290.A-Z Non-official. Codification scientifique. Restatements (e. g. the opinio juris). By author, A-Z

1290.B58 Bluntschli, Johann Casper, 1808-1881. Das moderne Völkerrecht der civilisierten Staaten als Rechtsbuch dargestellt (1868)

1290.D66 Domin-Petrusevec, Alphonse de. Precise d'un Code du Droit international (1861)

1290.D86 Duplessix, E. La loi des nations: projet d'institution d'un autorite nationale, legislative, administrative, judiciaire: projet de code de droit international public (1906)

1290.F54 Field, David Dudley (1805-1894). Draft outlines of an International Code (1872)

1290.F56 Fiore, P. Il diritto internazionale codificato e la sua sanzione giuridica (1890/1915)

1290.I68 Internoscia, Jerome. New Code of International Law (1911)

1290.L49 Levi, Leone. International law with materials for a Code of International law (1887)

1290.L54 Lieber, Francis. Laws of War (1863)

1290.P47 Pessoa, Epitacio. Projecto de codigo de direito internacional publico (1911)

General works

1292 Early (to 1920)

By language

1293 English

1293.5 French

1294 German

1294.5 Italian

1295 Japanese

1295.5 Russian

Codification of the law of nations. International law making
General works
By language -- Continued
1296 Spanish. Portuguese
1296.A-Z Other languages, A-Z
The law of treaties. System of treaty law
Including works on treaty making
Intergovernmental congresses and conferences. By name of the congress or conference
United Nations conferences
United Nations Conference on the Law of Treaties, 1968-1969
1298 Serials
1298.2 Monographs. By date
1298.23.A-Z Other United Nations Conferences. By name, A-Z
Under each:
.xA12-.xA199 Serials
.xA3 Monographs. By date
1298.23.U54 United Nations Conference on the Law of Treaties between States and International Organizations or between International Organizations, 1986
1298.3 Treaties and other international agreements. Conventions. Declarations. By date of signature
e. g.
Vienna Convention on the Law of Treaties, 1969
1299 Other official acts
Including notifications, protests, renunciations
1301 General works
1301.2 Typology
Including alliances, guaranty treaties, treaties of neutrality, etc.
1301.3 Treaty-making power
1301.5 Parties and third parties to the treaty. Multilateralism and bilateralism
1302 Form and parts of the treaty
Including final acts, protocols, accessions, etc.
1302.3 Signature. Ratification. Reservation. Registration
Validity and nullity. Invalidity
1302.5 General works
1303 Entering into force. Treaty compliance and enforcement. Pacta sunt servanda
For enforcement regimes see KZ6350+
1303.3 Expiration. Voidance. Cancellation. Suspension. Termination
1303.4 Revision. Renewal. Reconfirmation
1304 Interpretation of treaties. Rules of interpretation
<1305-1317.5> Political theory. Scope of international relations. Diplomacy
see JZ1305+

International cooperation through international regimes

1318 General works

Regime theory and analysis of regime formation

<1319> General

see JZ1319

Interdependence and transnationalism. Domestic dimensions

<1320> General

see JZ1320

National self-determination see KZ1269

<1320.3> National self-interest

see JZ1320.3

<1320.4> World citizenship

see JZ1320.4

<1320.5> Principle of good neighbourliness. Global neighbourhood

see JZ1320.5

<1320.7> Interregionalism. Transregionalism

see JZ1320.7

International legal regimes

Class here theoretical works on non-hierarchical legal regimes, i.e. collective self-regulation, or institutionalized co-operation for conflict management agreed upon by states in order to govern their conduct, and control their activities

For regimes limited by subject (specialized regimes), see the subject, e. g. K3891+, High-seas fisheries regimes; K3581+, Environmental regimes; KZ5615+, Arms control and disarmament regimes; K3236+, Human rights, etc.

1321 General works

Intergovernmental legal regimes governing the global commons

Class here theoretical works on governance of spaces beyond the limits of national jurisdiction

Including comparative works on specialized regimes governing Antarctica, the high seas, sea bed (and subsoil), and outer space combined

For works on a particular specialized regime, see the subject e. g. KWX, Antarctic Legal Regime; KZA1002+, Legal regimes governing the oceans; KZD1002+, Legal regimes governing space and outer space

Cf. KZ3673 Internationalized territory

1322 General works

Commons regime concepts and doctrines

1323 Common heritage of mankind regime

1323.5 Free access to the commons regime (Res communis. Res publica)

International cooperation through international regimes
International legal regimes
Intergovernmental legal regimes governing the global commons -- Continued
<1324-1327> International cooperation and diplomacy defined by subject areas
see JZ1324+
Ancient history and theory
General works see KZ1242
Ancient (Oriental) states see KL2+
Greece, Rhodian law see KL4101+
Rome. Ius gentium. Ius sacrum see KJA3320+
Early/Medieval development to ca. 1900. Ius Naturae et Gentium
For political and diplomatic history, or political and military/naval history, see the periods in the pertinent classes, e. g. D217
For the Consolat de mar (Consulate of the sea) see K1163.C6
For the Laws of Oléron see K1163.O4
For the Laws of Trani see K1163.T7
For individual publicists see KZ2064+
General works see KZ1242
To 1648
1328 General works
1328.2 Treaty of Verdun, 843 (Table K5)
1329.3 Treaty of Paris, 1258
For historical works on the Peace of Paris, 1258 see DC91.3
1329.8.A-Z Other treaties, alliances, etc. By name, A-Z
1329.8.A77 Treaty of Arras, 1435
For historical works on the Congress and Peace of Arras see DC102.535
1329.8.B74 Treaty of Bretigny, 1360
For historical works on the Peace of Bretigny see DC99.5.B7
1329.8.C36 Treaty of Cambrai, 1529
For historical works on the Peace of Cambrai (Ladies' Peace), 1529 see DC113.5
1329.8.C38 Treaty of Cateau-Cambrésis, 1559
For historical works on the Peace of Cateau-Cambrésis, 1559 see DC114
1329.8.M33 Treaty of Madrid, 1526
For historical works on the Peace of Madrid, 1526 see DC113.5
1329.8.T76 Treaty of Troyes, 1420
For historical works on the Peace of Troyes, 1420 see DC101.5.T7

Early/Medieval development to ca. 1900. Ius Naturae et Gentium -- Continued
Peace of Westphalia to the French Revolution (1648-1789)
Including treaties concluded during the Thirty Years' War, 1618-1648
1330 General works
Treaty of Lübeck, 1629
1330.5 The instrument (Table K5)
1330.7.A-Z Special topics, A-Z
1330.7.E3 Edict of restitution, 1629
1330.9 Truce of Ulm, 1647 (Table K5)
Peace of Westphalia. The treaties of Münster and Osnabrück, 1648
1331 Instrumentum pacis Monasteriense, 1648 (Table K5)
1333.A-Z Special topics, A-Z
1333.C94 Cuius regio eius religio principle
1333.3 Treaty of Breda, 1667 (Table K5)
1333.32 Treaty of Aix-la-Chapelle, 1668 (Table K5)
1333.4 Treaty of Nijmegen, 1678-1679 (Table K5)
1333.5 Treaty of Ryswick, 1697 (Table K5)
Treaty of Utrecht, 1713
Including related treaties and alliances
Cf. D283.5 History (General)
1334 The instrument, 1713 (Table K5)
1335.3.A-Z Special topics, A-Z
1335.3.S63 Spanish succession
1335.5 Treaty of Rastatt and Baden, 1714 (Table K5)
Treaty of Paris, 1763
Cf. D297 History (General)
1336 The instrument, 1763 (Table K5)
1338.A-Z Special topics, A-Z
1339.A-Z Other treaties, alliances, etc. By name, A-Z
1339.A59 Treaty of Aix-la-Chapelle, 1748
1339.F66 Family pact of Fontainebleau, 1743
1339.H36 Treaty of Hanover, 1725
1339.P37 Family pact of Paris, 1761
1339.Q83 Quadruple Alliance, 1718
1339.S48 Treaty of Seville, 1729
1339.V47 Treaty of Versailles, 1783
French Revolution to the American Civil War (1789-1861)
1345 General works
1346 Congress of Rastatt, 1797-1799
1346.3 Congress of Châtillon-sur-Seine, 1814
1347 Treaty of Ghent, 1814 (Table K5)
1348 Treaty of Paris, 1814 (Table K5)

Early/Medieval development to ca. 1900. Ius Naturae et Gentium
French Revolution to the American Civil War (1789-1861) -- Continued
1355 Congress of Vienna, 1814-1815
For legal forks on the Holy Alliance Treaty, 1815, including texts of the treaty and related works see KZ1358+
1355.5 Treaty of Paris, 1815. The Instrument, 1815 (Table K5)
Holy Alliance Treaty, 1815
1358 The instrument, 1815 (Table K5)
1358.3 Declaration of England against acts and projects of the Holy Alliance, 1821
1361 Congress of Troppau, 1820
1363 Congress of Laibach, 1821
1365 Congress of Verona, 1822
1367 Congress of Panama, 1826
1367.5 Quadruple (Alliance) Treaty, 1834 (Table K5)
1369 Treaty of Paris, 1856 (Table K5)
For Declaration of Paris, 1856 see KZ6550
1370.A-Z Other treaties, alliances, etc. By name, A-Z
1370.I56-Z Ionian Islands Treaty, 1815
American Civil War to the First Conference of the Hague (1861-1899)
1373 General works
St. Petersburg Declaration, 1868 see KZ5637
Treaty of London, 1871
1379 The instrument, 1871 (Table K5)
1380.A-Z Special topics, A-Z
1380.T74 Treaty obligations
Brussels Conference, 1874 see KZ6381+
1383 Treaty of Berlin, 1878 (Table K5)
1384 Triple Alliance, 1882
1385 Berlin West Africa Conference, 1884-1885
Cf. DT31+ Partition of Africa
Cf. DT652 Congo (General works)
1386 Treaty of Frankfort, 1871 (Franco-German War, 1870-1871) (Table K5)
Pan-American Congress, 1889-1890
1387 General works
1387.2 Pan-American Union, 1890
For later developments, e. g. the International American Conference (1889-1948), and Inter-American Conference (1948-1970) see KZ6034.A+
Cf. F1404+ Latin America
Treaty of Paris, 1898 (Spanish-American War, 1898)

Early/Medieval development to ca. 1900. Ius Naturae et Gentium

American Civil War to the First Conference of the Hague (1861-1899)

Treaty of Paris, 1898 (Spanish-American War, 1898) -- Continued

1389 The instrument (Table K5)

1390.A-Z Special topics, A-Z

Periods after Hague and Geneva Conferences and conventions (1899-)

see the subject, e. g. KZ6464+ Geneva Convention, July 6, 1906 (Relief of sick and wounded in war)

Diplomatic and consular service

For legal works on the diplomatic and consular services of a particular jurisdiction, see the jurisdiction, e.g. KF5112+ United States

1405 General works

1427 Diplomatic protection of citizens abroad

Publicists. Writers on public international law

Class here comprehensive theoretical treatises on the Law of Nations, and general works including contemporary and recent criticism on such works

For works on a particular subject, see the subject, e. g. KZA1348 Grotius, Mare Liberum

2064 Collections. Selections

To 18th century. By author or title

2071 Alonso de la Vera Cruz, fray, ca. 1507-1584 (Table K3)

2072 Ayala, Balthazar, 1548-1584 (Table K3)

2072.A3A-.A3Z Individual works. By title

e.g.

De jure et officiis bellicis et disciplina militari libri III (1582) see KZ6385

2073 Belli, Pierino, 1502-1575 (Table K3)

2075 Bodin, Jean, 1530-1596 (Table K3)

2081 Brunus, Conradus, ca. 1491-1563 (Table K3)

2083 Brunus - Cumberland

Subarrange each author by Table K4

2083.C37 Casas, Bartholomé de las, bp. of Chiapa, 1474-1566 (Table K4)

2083.C68 Covarrubias y Leyva, Diego de, 1512-1577 (Table K4)

2085 Cumberland, Richard, 1631-1718 (Table K3)

2086 Cumberland - Gentili

Subarrange each author by Table K4

2087 Gentili, Alberico, 1552-1608 (Table K3 modified)

2087.A3A-.A3Z Individual works. By title

e.g.

Early/Medieval development to ca. 1900. Ius Naturae et Gentium
Publicists. Writers on public international law
To 18th century. By author or title
Gentili, Alberico, 1552-1608
Individual works. By title -- Continued
Commentationes de jure belli (1588 and 1589) see KZ6385
De jure belli libri tres (1598) see KZ6385
De legationibus (1585)
2089 Goudelin, Pierre, 1550-1619 (Table K3)
Grotius, Hugo, 1583-1645
2093.A2 Collected works. Opera omnia. Selections. By date
2093.A3A-.A3Z Individual works. By title
e. g.
De jure praedae see KZ6600
De jure belli ac pacis libri tres
Mare liberum see KZA1348
2093.A6-Z Biography. Criticism
Including early (contemporary) works
2107 Grotius - Leibnitz
Subarrange each author by Table K4
2107.H62 Hobbes, Thomas, 1588-1679 (Table K4)
2107.K5 Kirchner, Hermann, 1562-1620 (Table K4)
2110 Leibnitz, Gottfried Wilhelm, Freiherr von, 1646-1716 (Table K3)
2112 Loccenius, Johan, 1598-1677 (Table K3)
2116 Machiavelli, Niccolo, 1469-1527 (Table K3)
2117 Machiavelli - Molloy
Subarrange each author by Table K4
2119 Molloy, Charles, 1646-1690 (Table K3)
2125 Peck, Pierre, 1529-1589 (Table K3)
2136 Pufendorf, Samuel, Freiherr von, 1632-1694 (Table K3 modified)
Cf. JC156 Political theory
2136.A3A-.A3Z Individual works. By title
e. g. Elementa jurisprudentiae universalis (1666); De jure naturae et gentium libri octo (1672); De officio hominis et civis juxta legem naturalem (1673)
2141 Rachel, Samuel, 1628-1691 (Table K3 modified)
2141.A3A-.A3Z Individual works. By title
e. g. De jure naturae et gentium (1676)
2144 Santorem, Pedro de, 16th/17th cent. (Table K3)
2147 Selden, John, 1584-1654 (Table K3 modified)
2147.A3A-.A3Z Individual works. By title
De juri naturali et gentium, juxta disciplinam Ebraeorum, libri septem (1665) see KBM524.15

Early/Medieval development to ca. 1900. Ius Naturae et Gentium
Publicists. Writers on public international law
To 18th century. By author or title
Selden, John, 1584-1654
Individual works. By title -- Continued
Mare clausum see KZA1340

2149 Sepúlveda, Juan Ginés de, 1490-1573 (Table K3)
2151 Simon, Johann Georg, ca. 1636-1696 (Table K3)
2156 Suárez, Francisco, 1548-1617 (Table K3)
2157 Suárez - Vitoria
Subarrange each author by Table K4
2157.T49 Textor, Johann Wolfgang, 1638-1701 (Table K4)
Including Synopsis juris gentium (1680)
2157.T56 Thomas Aquinas, Saint, 1225?-1274 (Table K4)
2157.V45 Veltheim, Valentin, 1645-1700 (Table K4)
2159 Vitoria, Francisco, 1480-1546 (Table K3)
2163 Wicquefort, Abraham de, 1606-1682 (Table K3)
2164 Ziegler, Kaspar, 1621-1690 (Table K3 modified)
2164.A3A-.A3Z Individual works. By title
e. g. In Hugonis Grotii De jure belli ac pacis
2181 Zouch, Richard, 1590-1661 (Table K3)
18th century. By author or title
Subarrange each author by Table K3 or K4
English
2220 A - Bentham
Subarrange each author by Table K4
2221 Bentham, Jeremy, 1718-1832 (Table K3)
2223 Bentham - Fulbeck
Subarrange each author by Table K4
2225 Fulbeck, William, 1560-1603? (Table K3)
2227 Fulbeck - Rutherforth
Subarrange each author by Table K4
2227.H98 Hutcheson, Francis, 1694-1746. System of moral philosophy (1755) (Table K4)
2231 Rutherforth, Thomas, 1712-1771. Institutes of natural law (1754-1756) (Table K3)
2233 Rutherforth - Z
Subarrange each author by Table K4
Dutch
2242 A - Bijnkershoek
Subarrange each author by Table K4
2243 Bijnkershoek, Cornelis van, 1673-1743 (Table K3 modified)
2243.A3A-.A3Z Individual works. By title
e. g. De foro legatorum (1721); Questionum juris publici libri duo (1737)

Early/Medieval development to ca. 1900. Ius Naturae et Gentium
Publicists. Writers on public international law
18th century. By author or title
Dutch
Bijnkershoek, Cornelis van, 1673-1743
Individual works. By title -- Continued
De dominio maris see KZA1340

2245 Bijnkershoek - Z
Subarrange each author by Table K4

2245.N63 Noest, Gerard, fl. 1753 (Table K4)

2260-2276 French

2260 A - Mably
Subarrange each author by Table K4

2260.B37 Barbeyrac, Jean, 1674-1744 (Table K4)

2261 Mably, Gabriel Bonnot de, 1709-1785 (Table K3)

2266 Mably - Montesquieu
Subarrange each author by Table K4

2271 Montesquieu, Charles de Secondat, baron de, 1689-1755 (Table K3)

2273 Montesquieu - Neytron
Subarrange each author by Table K4

2274 Neyron, Pierre Joseph, 1740-1810 (Table K3)

2276 Neyron - Z
Subarrange each author by Table K4

German

2304 Achenwall, Gottfried, 1719-1772 (Table K3)

2305 Achenwall - Glafey
Subarrange each author by Table K4

2305.B84 Buddeus, Joannes Franciscus, 1667-1729 (Table K4)

2305.C62 Cocceji, Heinrich von, 1644-1719 (Table K4)

2305.C63 Cocceji, Samuel, Freiherr von, 1679-1755 (Table K4 modified)

2305.C63A3-.C63A39 Individual works. By title
e. g. Samuelis l.b. de Cocceji ... Introductio ad ... Grotium illustratum (1748)

2305.E55 Eggers, Christian Ulrich Detlev, Freiherr von, 1758-1813 (Table K4)

2306 Glafey, Adam Friedrich, 1692-1753 (Table K3)

2308 Glafey - Günther
Subarrange each author by Table K4

2311 Günther, Karl Gottlob, 1752-1832 (Table K3)

2313 Günther - Heineccius
Subarrange each author by Table K4

2314 Heineccius, Johann Gottlieb, 1681-1741 (Table K3 modified)

Early/Medieval development to ca. 1900. Ius Naturae et Gentium
Publicists. Writers on public international law
18th century. By author or title
German
Heineccius, Johann Gottlieb, 1681-1741 -- Continued
2314.A3A-.A3Z Individual works. By title
e. g. Praelectiones academicae in Hugonis Grotii De jure belli ac pacis libros III (1744)
2316 Heineccius - Kant
Subarrange each author by Table K4
2322 Kant, Immanuel, 1724-1804 (Table K3)
2323 Kant - Martens
Subarrange each author by Table K4
2323.K75 Köhler, Heinrich, 1685-1737 (Table K4)
Martens, Georg Friedrich von see KZ2814
Martens, Karl, Freiherr von, 1790-1863 see KZ2814.5
2326 Martens - Moser
Subarrange each author by Table K4
2328 Moser, Friedrich Carl, Freiherr von, 1723-1798 (Table K3)
2333 Moser, Johann Jakob, 1701-1785 (Table K3 modifed)
2333.A3A-.A3Z Individual works. By title
e. g.
Grundsätze des jetzt üblichen Völkerrechts in Friedenszeiten (1750)
Grundsätze des jetzt üblichen Völkerrechts in Kriegszeiten (1752)
Versuch des neuesten europäischen Völkerrechts in Friedens-und Kriegszeiten (1777-1780)
2334 Moser - Ompteda
Subarrange each author by Table K4
2335 Ompteda, Dietrich Heinrich Ludwig, Freiherr von, 1746-1803 (Table K3)
2339 Ompteda - Thomasius
Subarrange each author by Table K4
2339.R75 Römer, Carl Heinrich von, 1760-1798 (Table K4)
2344 Thomasius, Christian, 1655-1728 (Table K3 modified)
2344.A3A-.A3Z Individual works. By title
e. g. Fundamenta juris naturae et gentium (1705)
2346 Thomasius - Wolff
Subarrange each author by Table K4
2346.W45 Weidler, Johann Friedrich, 1691-1755 (Table K4)
2346.W47 Wenck, Friedrich August Wilhelm, 1741-1810 (Table K4)
2347 Wolff, Christian, Freiherr von, 1679-1754 (Table K3 modified)

Early/Medieval development to ca. 1900. Ius Naturae et Gentium
Publicists. Writers on public international law
18th century. By author or title
German
Wolff, Christian, Freiherr von, 1679-1754 -- Continued
2347.A3A-.A3Z Individual works. By title
e.g. Institutiones juris naturae et gentium (1750); Jus gentium methodo scientifica pertractatum (1749)
2349 Wolff - Z
Subarrange each author by Table K4
2349.Z35 Zechin, Johann Karl Ludwig, b. 1774 (Table K4)
Italian
2370 A - Azuni
Subarrange each author by Table K4
2371 Azuni, D.A. (Dominico Alberto), 1749-1827 (Table K3)
2373 Azuni - Lampredi
Subarrange each author by Table K4
2374 Lampredi, Giovanni Maria, 1732-1793 (Table K3)
2379 Lampredi - Z
Subarrange each author by Table K4
Spanish and Portuguese
2388 A - P
Subarrange each author by Table K4
2388.M87 Muriel, Domingo (Morelli), 1718-1795 (Table K4)
2388.O56 Olmeda y Leon, Joseph de, 1740-1805 (Table K4)
2388.O77 Ortega y Cotes, Ignacio José de (Table K4)
2389 P - Z
Subarrange each author by Table K4
Scandinavian
2391 A - Hübner
Subarrange each author by Table K4
Eggers see KZ2305.E55
2394 Hübner, Martin, 1723-1795 (Table K3)
2395 Hübner - Z
Subarrange each author by Table K4
Swiss
2400 A - Burlamaqui
Subarrange each author by Table K4
2401 Burlamaqui, Jean Jacques, 1694-1748 (Table K3)
2406 Burlamaqui - Vattel
Subarrange each author by Table K4
2406.F45 Félice, Fortuné Bartholémy de, 1723-1789 (Table K4)
2414 Vattel, Emer de, 1714-1767 (Table K3)
2420 Vattel - Z
Subarrange each author by Table K4

Early/Medieval development to ca. 1900. Ius Naturae et Gentium
Publicists. Writers on public international law
18th century. By author or title -- Continued
2435.A-Z Other nationals. By publicist, A-Z
Subarrange each author by Table K4
19th century. By author or title
Subarrange each author by Table K3 or K4
American
2451 A - Davis, C.
Subarrange each author by Table K4
2451.B68 Bowen, Herbert Wolcott, 1856-1927 (Table K4)
2455 Davis, Cushman Kellog, 1838-1900 (Table K3)
2458 Davis, George B. (George Breckenridge), 1847-1914 (Table K3)
2460 Davis - Field
Subarrange each author by Table K4
2460.D73 Duane, William John, 1780-1865 (Table K4)
2464 Field, D.D. (Table K3)
2467 Gallaudet, Edward Miner, 1837-1917 (Table K3)
2469 Gallaudet - Halleck
Subarrange each author by Table K4
2469.G28 Gardner, Daniel, 1799-1836 (Table K4)
2469.G45 Glenn, Edwin F. (Forbes), 1857-1926 (Table K4)
2475 Halleck, H.W. (Henry Wager), 1815-1872 (Table K3)
2478 Kent, James, 1763-1847 (Table K3)
2480 Kent - Lawrence, W.B.
Subarrange each author by Table K4
2481 Lawrence, William Beach, 1800-1881 (Table K3)
2483 Lawrence - Snow
Subarrange each author by Table K4
2483.L64 Lieber, Francis, 1800-1872 (Table K4)
2483.P76 Pomeroy, John Norton, 1828-1885 (Table K4)
2486 Snow, Freeman, d. 1894? (Table K3)
2489 Story, Joseph, 1779-1845 (Table K3)
2492 Wharton, William Fisher, 1847-1919 (Table K3)
2495 Wheaton, Henry, 1785-1848 (Table K3)
2498 Woolsey, Theodore Dwight, 1801-1889 (Table K3)
2500 Woolsey - Z
Subarrange each author by Table K4
2502.A-Z Dutch, A-Z
Subarrange each author by Table K4
English
2503 A - Amos
Subarrange each author by Table K4
2505 Amos, Sheldon, 1835-1886 (Table K3)

Early/Medieval development to ca. 1900. Ius Naturae et Gentium
Publicists. Writers on public international law
19th century. By author or title
English -- Continued

2507 Amos - Creasy
Subarrange each author by Table K4
2514 Creasy, Edward Shepherd, Sir, 1812-1878 (Table K3)
2523 Creasy - Hall
Subarrange each author by Table K4
2523.G66 Griffith, William, 1830-1898 (Table K4)
2524 Hall, William Edward, 1836-1894 (Table K3)
2527 Hertslet, Edward, Sir, 1824-1902 (Table K3)
2529 Hertslet - Holland
Subarrange each author by Table K4
2531 Holland, Thomas Erskine, Sir, 1835-1926 (Table K3)
2533 Holland - Hosack
Subarrange each author by Table K4
2538 Hosack, John, 1809-1887 (Table K3)
2540 Hosack - Lawrence
Subarrange each author by Table K4
2542 Lawrence, Thomas Joseph, 1849-1919 (Table K3)
2545 Levi, Leone, 1821-1888 (Table K3)
2548 Lorimer, James, 1818-1890 (Table K3)
2550 Lorimer - MacKintosh
Subarrange each author by Table K4
2552 MacKintosh (Table K3)
2554 Mackintosh - Maine
Subarrange each author by Table K4
2555 Maine, Henry James Sumner, Sir, 1822-1888 (Table K3)
2558 Manning, William Oke (Table K3)
2564 Manning - Phillimore
Subarrange each author by Table K4
2564.M55 Miller, William G. (Table K4)
2565 Phillimore, Robert, Sir, 1810-1885 (Table K3)
2567 Phillimore - Polson
Subarrange each author by Table K4
2572 Polson, Archer (Table K3)
2574 Polson - Stowell
Subarrange each author by Table K4
2579 Scott, William, Baron Stowell, 1745-1836 (Table K3)
2580 Stowell - Twiss
Subarrange each author by Table K4
2582 Twiss, Travers, Sir, 1809-1897 (Table K3)
2584 Twiss - Ward
Subarrange each author by Table K4

KZ

Early/Medieval development to ca. 1900. Ius Naturae et Gentium
Publicists. Writers on public international law
19th century. By author or title
English
Twiss - Ward -- Continued
2584.W35 Walker, Thomas Alfred, 1862-1935 (Table K4)
2585 Ward, R.P. (Robert Plumer), 1765-1846 (Table K3)
2588 Westlake, John, 1828-1913 (Table K3)
2590 Westlake - Wildman
Subarrange each author by Table K4
2592 Wildman, Richard, 1802-1881 (Table K3)
2594 Wildman - Z
Subarrange each author by Table K4
French
Including Belgian publicists or titles
2607 A - Bonfils
Subarrange each author by Table K4
2608 Bonfils, Henry Joseph François Xavier, 1835-1897 (Table K3)
2613 Bonfils - Cauchy
Subarrange each author by Table K4
2613.B88 Bry, Georges Ernest, b. 1847 (Table K4)
2615 Cauchy, Eugène François, 1802-1877 (Table K3)
2616 Cauchy - Cussy
Subarrange each author by Table K4
2616.C47 Chrétien, Alfred Marie Victor (Table K4)
2624 Cussy, Ferdinand de Cornot, Baron, 1795-1866 (Table K3)
2626 Cussy - Despagnet
Subarrange each author by Table K4
2641 Despagnet, Frantz Clément René, 1857-1906 (Table K3)
2643 Despagnet - Fauchille
Subarrange each author by Table K4
2651 Fauchille, Paul, 1858-1926 (Table K3)
2656 Fauchille - Féraud
Subarrange each author by Table K4
2658 Féraud-Giraud, L.-J.-D. (Louis-Joseph-Delphine), b. 1819 (Table K3)
2660 Féraud - Funck
Subarrange each author by Table K4
2668 Funck-Brentano, Theophile, 1830-1906 (Table K3)
2672 Garden, Guillaume, Comte de, 1796-1872 (Table K3)
2673 Garden - Laveleye
Subarrange each author by Table K4

Early/Medieval development to ca. 1900. Ius Naturae et Gentium
Publicists. Writers on public international law
19th century. By author or title
French
Garden - Laveleye -- Continued
2673.G47 Gérard de Rayneval, J.-M. (Joseph-Mathias), 1736-1812 (Table K4)
2673.G66 Gondon, J.J.B. (Table K4)
2687 Laveleye, Emile de, 1822-1892 (Table K3)
2701 Laveleye - Nys
Subarrange each author by Table K4
2701.L48 Leseur, Paul (Table K4)
2701.M53 Michel, Claude Louis Samson, 1754-1811 (Table K4)
2702 Nys, Ernst, b. 1851 (Table K3)
2704 Nys - Piédelièvre
Subarrange each author by Table K4
2714 Piédelièvre, Robert, b. 1859 (Table K3)
2716 Piédelièvre - Pradier
Subarrange each author by Table K4
2725 Pradier-Fodéré, P. (Paul), 1827-1904 (Table K3)
2728 Proudhon, P.-J. (Pierre-Joseph), 1809-1865 (Table K3)
2730 Proudhon - Renault
Subarrange each author by Table K4
2735 Renault, Louis, 1843-1918 (Table K3)
2737 Renault - Rivier
Subarrange each author by Table K4
2739 Rivier, Alphonse (Pierre Octave), 1835-1898 (Table K3)
2742 Rolin-Jacquemyns, Gustave Henry Auge Hippolyt, 1835-1902 (Table K3)
2745 Rouard de Card, E. (Edgard), b. 1835 (Table K3)
2747 Rouard - Sorel
Subarrange each author by Table K4
2751 Sorel, Albert, 1842-1906 (Table K3)
2753 Sorel - Z
Subarrange each author by Table K4
German
Including Swiss and Austrian publicists or titles
2774 A - Bluntschli
Subarrange each author by Table K4
2775 Bluntschli, Johann Caspar, 1808-1881 (Table K3)
2778 Bulmerincq, August von, 1822-1890 (Table K3)
2781 Gagern, Heinrich, Freiherr von, 1799-1880 (Table K3)
2783 Gagern - Gz
Subarrange each author by Table K4
2783.G37 Gareis, Karl, 1844-1923 (Table K4)

Early/Medieval development to ca. 1900. Ius Naturae et Gentium
Publicists. Writers on public international law
19th century. By author or title
German -- Continued

2786 H - Heffter
Subarrange each author by Table K4
2786.H37 Hartmann, Adolf, fl. 1874-1906 (Table K4)
2787 Heffter, August Wilhelm, 1796-1880 (Table K3)
2789 Heffter - Holtzendorff
Subarrange each author by Table K4
2789.H45 Heilborn, Paul, 1861-1932 (Table K4)
2791 Holtzendorff, Franz von, 1829-1889 (Table K3)
2793 Holtzendorff - Kaltenborn
Subarrange each author by Table K4
2797 Kaltenborn von Stachau, Carl, Baron, 1817-1866 (Table K3)
2799 Kaltenborn - Kamptz
Subarrange each author by Table K4
2801 Kamptz (Table K3)
2804 Klüber, Johann Ludwig, 1762-1837 (Table K3)
2806 Klüber - Lasson
Subarrange each author by Table K4
2811 Lasson, Adolf, 1832-1917 (Table K3)
2814 Martens, G. F. de (Georg Friedrich), 1756-1821 (Table K3)
2814.5 Martens, Karl, Freiherr von, 1790-1863 (Table K3)
2817 Neumann, Leopold, Freiherr von, 1811-1888 (Table K3)
2819 Neumann - Oppenheim
Subarrange each author by Table K4
2821 Oppenheim, Heinrich Bernhard, 1819-1880 (Table K3)
2824 Oppenheim - Saalfeld
Subarrange each author by Table K4
2824.P65 Pölitz, Karl Heinrich Ludwig, 1772-1838 (Table K4)
2824.Q93 Quaritsch, August (Table K4)
2824.R48 Resch, Peter, b. 1850 (Table K4)
2826 Saalfeld, Friedrich, 1785-1834 (Table K3)
2828 Saalfeld - Schlief
Subarrange each author by Table K4
2833 Schlief, Eugen - Schmalz
Subarrange each author by Table K4
2833.S45 Schlözer, Christian von, 1774-1831 (Table K4)
2834 Schmalz, Theodor Anton Heinrich, 1760-1831 (Table K3)
2836 Schmalz - Schulze
Subarrange each author by Table K4

Early/Medieval development to ca. 1900. Ius Naturae et Gentium
Publicists. Writers on public international law
19th century. By author or title
German
Schmalz - Schulze -- Continued
2836.S45 Schmelzing, Julius (Table K4)
2841 Stoerk, Felix, 1851-1908 (Table K3)
2843 Stoerk - Z
Subarrange each author by Table K4
2843.U6 Ullmann, Emanuel Ritter von, 1843-1913 (Table K4)
Greek
2844 A - Saripolos
Subarrange each author by Table K4
2845 Saripolos, Nicolaos I. (Nicolaos Ioannou), 1817-1887 (Table K3)
2847 Saripolos - Z
Subarrange each author by Table K4
Italian
2857 A - Carnazza
Subarrange each author by Table K4
2858 Carnazza Amari, Giuseppe, b. 1837? (Table K3)
2860 Carnazza - Casanova
Subarrange each author by Table K4
2862 Casanova, Ludovico, 1799-1853 (Table K3)
2865 Celli (Table K3)
2868 Contuzzi, Francesco Paolo, b. 1855 (Table K3)
2870 Contuzzi - Del Bon
Subarrange each author by Table K4
2872 Del Bon, Antonio, b. 1832 (Table K3)
2875 Esperson (Table K3)
2878 Ferrero Gola, Andrea (Table K3)
2881 Fiore, Pasquale, 1837-1914 (Table K3)
2883 Fiore - Grasso
Subarrange each author by Table K4
2887 Grasso, Giacomo, b. 1859 (Table K3)
2889 Grasso - Macri
Subarrange each author by Table K4
2889.L39 Lazzarini, Alessandro (Table K4)
2894 Macri, Giacomo, b. 1831 (Table K3)
2897 Mamiani della Rovere, Terenzio, Conte, 1799-1885 (Table K3)
2899 Mamiani - Morello
Subarrange each author by Table K4
2904 Morello, Paolo (Table K3)
2910 Morello - Pertile
Subarrange each author by Table K4

Early/Medieval development to ca. 1900. Ius Naturae et Gentium
Publicists. Writers on public international law
19th century. By author or title
Italian
Morello - Pertile -- Continued
2910.O55 Olivi, Luigi, 1847-1911 (Table K4)
2914 Pertile, Antonio, 1830-1895 (Table K3)
2917 Pierantoni, Augusto, 1840-1911 (Table K3)
2919 Pierantoni - Sandonà
Subarrange each author by Table K4
2924 Sandonà, Guiuseppe (Table K3)
2926 Sandonà - Schiattarella
Subarrange each author by Table K4
2928 Schiattarella, Raffaele (Table K3)
2930 Schiattarella - Z
Subarrange each author by Table K4
Russian
2940 A - Bergholm
Subarrange each author by Table K4
2941 Bergholm (Table K3)
2943 Bergholm - Martens
Subarrange each author by Table K4
Bulmerincq see KZ2778
2951 Martens, Fedor Fedorovich, 1845-1909 (Table K3)
2953 Martens - Z
Subarrange each author by Table K4
Scandinavian
2954 A - Matzen
Subarrange each author by Table K4
2955 Matzen, Henning, 1840-1910 (Table K3)
2957 Matzen - Tetens
Subarrange each author by Table K4
2961 Tetens, Peter Jacobsen, 1797-1859 (Table K3)
2963 Tetens - Z
Subarrange each author by Table K4
Spanish and Portuguese
Including Latin American publicists or titles
2966 A - Alcorta
Subarrange each author by Table K4
2967 Alcorta, Amancio, 1842-1902 (Table K3)
2969 Alcorta - Arenal
Subarrange each author by Table K4
2975 Arenal de García Carrasco, Concepción, 1820-1893 (Table K3)
2977 Arenal - Bello
Subarrange each author by Table K4

Early/Medieval development to ca. 1900. Ius Naturae et Gentium
Publicists. Writers on public international law
19th century. By author or title
Spanish and Portuguese -- Continued

2978 Bello, Andrés, 1781-1865 (Table K3)
2980 Bello - Calvo
Subarrange each author by Table K4
2980.C35 Calcaño (Table K4)
2984 Calvo, Carlos, 1824-1906 (Table K3)
2986 Calvo - Ferrater
Subarrange each author by Table K4
2986.C78 Cruchaga Tocornal, Miguel, 1869- (Table K4)
2986.D54 Diez de Medina (Table K4)
2991 Ferrater, Estaban de, 1812-1873 (Table K3)
2994 Ferreira, Ramón, 1803-1874 (Table K3)
2996 Ferreira - Gestoso
Subarrange each author by Table K4
3001 Gestoso y Acosto, luis (Table K3)
3003 Gestoso - Labra
Subarrange each author by Table K4
3007 Labra y Cadrana, Rafael María de, 1841-1918 (Table K3)
3015 Labra - López Sánchez
Subarrange each author by Table K4
3015.L66 López, José Francisco (Table K4)
3017 López Sánchez, Pedro, d. 1881 (Table K3)
3019 López - Madiedo
Subarrange each author by Table K4
3021 Madiedo, Manuel María, b. 1818 (Table K3)
3027 Madiedo - Mozo
Subarrange each author by Table K4
3027.M55 Montúfar y Rivera Maestre, Lorenzo, 1823-1898 (Table K4)
3027.M67 Moreira de Almeida, José Augusto (Table K4)
3028 Mozo, Manuel J. (Table K3)
3030 Mozo - Olivart
Subarrange each author by Table K4
3034 Olivart, Ramón de Daimau y de Olivart, Marqués de, 1861-1928 (Table K3)
3036 Olivart - Pando
Subarrange each author by Table K4
3038 Pando, José María de, 1787-1840 (Table K3)
3040 Pando - Pinheiro
Subarrange each author by Table K4
3040.P47 Pérez Gomar, Gregorio, 1834-1885 (Table K4)
3041 Pinheiro-Ferreira (Table K3)

Early/Medieval development to ca. 1900. Ius Naturae et Gentium
Publicists. Writers on public international law
19th century. By author or title
Spanish and Portuguese -- Continued
3043 Pinheiro - Riquelme
Subarrange each author by Table K4
3043.P73 Pradier-Fodéré, Camille, 185? (Table K4)
3045 Riquelme, Antonio (Table K3)
3047.R4 Rodríguez Saráchaga, Oscar, 1867-1936 (Table K4)
3048 Seijas, Rafael Fernando (Table K3)
3050 Seijas - Torres Campos
Subarrange each author by Table K4
3055 Torres Campos, Manuel, 1850-1918 (Table K3)
3058 Tremosa y Nadal, Angel (Table K3)
3060 Tremosa - Z
Subarrange each author by Table K4
3085.A-Z Other nationals. By publicist, A-Z
Subarrange each author by Table K4
20th century
3092 Collections. Selections
Writers or titles on public international law
Subarrange each writer by Table K3 or K4
American
3110 A - Hershey
Subarrange each author by Table K4
3110.F68 Foulke, Roland Robert, 1874- (Table K4)
3110.H35 Hall, Arnold Bennett, 1881-1936 (Table K4)
3131 Hershey, Amos Shartle, 1867- (Table K3)
3140 Hershey - Maxey
Subarrange each author by Table K4
3140.H84 Hyde, Charles Chaney, 1837- (Table K4)
3140.J47 Jessup, Philip Caryl, 1897- (Table K4)
3151 Maxey, Edwin, 1869- (Table K3)
3160 Maxey - Scott
Subarrange each author by Table K4
3160.R4 Root, Elihu, 1845-1937 (Table K4)
3178 Scott, James Brown, 1866-1943 (Table K3)
3180 Scott - Taylor
Subarrange each author by Table K4
3180.S46 Singer, Berthold, 1860- (Table K4)
3180.S76 Stockton, Charles Herbert, 1845-1924 (Table K4)
3181 Taylor, Hannis, 1851-1922 (Table K3)
3185 Taylor - Wilson
Subarrange each author by Table K4
3191 Wilson, George Grafton, 1863- (Table K3)

20th century
Writers or titles on public international law
American -- Continued
3195 Wilson - Z
Subarrange each author by Table K4
English
Including Canadian authors or titles
3205 A - Baker
Subarrange each author by Table K4
3215 Baker - Birkenhead
Subarrange each author by Table K4
3215.B38 Baty, Thomas, 1869-1954 (Table K4)
3220 Birkenhead, Frederick Edwin Smith, (1st earl of) Baron, 1872-1930 (Table K3)
3225 Birkenhead - Oppenheim
Subarrange each author by Table K4
3225.B75 Brierly, James Leslie, 1881-1950 (Table K4)
3225.B87 Burns, Cecile Delisle, 1879-1942 (Table K4)
3225.L38 Lauterpacht, Hersch, Sir, 1897-1960 (Table K4)
3225.M38 McWhinney, Edward (Table K4)
3264 Oppenheim, Lassa Francis Lawrence, 1858-1919 (Table K3)
3275 Oppenheim - Smith
Subarrange each author by Table K4
3275.P53 Plater, Charles Dominic, 1875- (Table K4)
3275.S35 Schwarzenberger, Georg, 1908- (Table K4)
Smith, Frederick Edwin see KZ3220
3295 Smith - Z
Subarrange each author by Table K4
French
Including Belgian authors or titles
3310 A - Mérignhac
Subarrange each author by Table K4
3315 Mérignhac, Alexander Giraud Jacques Antoine, 1857- (Table K3)
3350 Mérignhac - Z
Subarrange each author by Table K4
3350.P56 Pinto, Roger (Table K4)
3350.R44 Reuter, Paul, 1911- (Table K4)
3350.R68 Rousseau, Charles E., 1902- (Table K4)
3350.V57 Visscher, Charles de (Table K4)
German
Including Swiss and Austro-Hungarian authors or titles
3375 A - Liszt
Subarrange each author by Table K4
3375.C93 Cybichowski, Zygmunt, 1879-1944 (Table K4)
3375.D35 Dahm, Georg, 1904-1963 (Table K4)

20th century
Writers or titles on public international law
German
A - Liszt -- Continued
3375.K45 Kelsen, Hans, b. 1881 (Table K4)
3375.K75 Kohler, Josef, 1849-1919 (Table K4)
3383 Liszt, Franz von, 1851-1919 (Table K3)
3390 Liszt - Z
Subarrange each author by Table K4
3390.N54 Niemeyer, Theodor, 1857- (Table K4)
3390.P65 Pohl, Heinrich, 1883-1931 (Table K4)
3390.S45 Schaeffer, Carl, 1871- (Table K4)
3390.S54 Schucking, W.M.A. (Walter Max Adrian), 1875-1935 (Table K4)
3390.S58 Seidl-Hohenveldern, Ignaz (Table K4)
3390.S87 Strupp, Karl, 1886-1940 (Table K4)
3390.V47 Verdross, Alfred, b. 1890 (Table K4)
3390.Z57 Zorn, Albert (Table K4)
3395.A-Z Italian, A-Z
Subarrange each author by Table K4
3395.A59 Anzilotti, Dionisio, 1869-1950 (Table K4)
3395.B35 Balladore-Pallieri, Giorgio, 1905- (Table K4)
3395.C25 Cassese, Antonio (Table K4)
3395.C27 Catellani, Enrico Levi, 1856-1940 (Table K4)
3395.D44 Diena, Guilio, b. 1865 (Table K4)
3395.L55 Lomonaco, Giovanni, b. 1848 (Table K4)
3395.Q93 Quadri, Rolando (Table K4)
3400.A-Z Spanish and Portuguese, A-Z
Subarrange each author by Table K4
Including Latin American authors or titles
3400.A33 Accioly, Hildebrando (Table K4)
3400.A53 Alcántara y García, Louis (Table K4)
3400.A68 Alvarez, Alejandro, 1868-1960 (Table K4)
3400.B27 Barros Jarpa, Ernesto, b. 1894 (Table K4)
3400.B38 Bevilaqua, Clovis, 1861-1944 (Table K4)
3400.B77 Bustamente y Siruén, Antonio Sánchez de, b. 1865 (Table K4)
3400.C86 Cunha, Joaquim Moreira da Silva (Table K4)
3400.D27 D'Estéfano Pisani, Miguel A. (Table K4)
3400.D54 Diez de Velaso Vallejo, Manuel (Table K4)
3400.F37 Fernández Prida, Joaquin, b. 1863 (Table K4)
3400.F56 Flores y Flores, José (Table K4)
3400.G27 García Álvarez, Manuel (Table K4)
3400.L55 Linares, Antonio, b. 1914 (Table K4)
3400.M387 Mello, Celso D. de Albyquerque, b. 1937 (Table K4)
3400.P58 Planas Suárez, Simon (Table K4)
3400.R85 Ruiz Moreno, Isidoro, b. 1876 (Table K4)

20th century
Writers or titles on public international law
Spanish and Portuguese, A-Z -- Continued
3400.S37 Sarmiento Laspiur, Eduardo (Table K4)
3400.S46 Sepúlveda, César (Table K4)
3405.A-Z Other nationals. By author or title, A-Z
Subarrange each author by Table K4
e. g.
3405.C548 Chou, Kêng-shêng, 1889- (Table K4)
3405.F5 Fleischer, Carl August (Table K4)
3405.J3 Jancović, Branimir M. (Table K4)
3405.J5 Jitta, D. Josephus (Daniël Josephus), 1854-1924 (Table K4)
3405.K642 Kozhevnikov, Fedor Ivanovich (Table K4)
3405.L5 Lisovski, Vadim Ivanovich (Table K4)
3405.P87 Puto, Arben (Table K4)
3405.R6 Ross, Alf, 1899- (Table K4)
3405.R66 Rosenne, Shabtai (Table K4)
3405.S54 Shubbar, Hikmat (Table K4)
3405.T23 Tabata, Shigejirō, 1911- (Table K4)
3405.T3 Tammes, A.J.P. (Table K4)
3405.T337 Taoka, Ryoichi, 1898- (Table K4)
3410 21st century
Class here general works on international law that were first published in the twenty-first century
For works on a particular subject, see the subject
For history of international law see KZ1242
Objects of the law of nations
Territory and its different parts
3670 General works
Concepts and principles
3673 Terra nullius territory
Including internationalized territories (global commons)
For theoretical works on legal regimes governing the global commons see KZ1322+
State territory. National jurisdiction
Including surface, subsoil, air space, and continental shelf
For territorial supremacy (sovereignty) see KZ4042
3675 General works
3678 Exterritoriality
3679 Acquisition and loss of territory
3679.5 Neighbourship and servitudes. Right of passage and transit
Boundaries. Delimitation of land, sea, and space boundaries
Cf. JC323 Political geography

Objects of the law of nations
Territory and its different parts
Boundaries. Delimitation of land, sea, and space boundaries -- Continued
Boundary treaties and other international agreements. Conventions see KZ176+
Boundary trials before the International Court of Justice see KZ1165
Boundary arbitration before an arbitration tribunal between two and more countries in a region see KZ238+
3684 General (Table K8)
3684.5.A-Z By region or country, A-Z
3685 Natural boundaries and artificial boundaries
Including mountains, rivers, lakes, etc.
For particular rivers, mountains, etc. as boundaries, see the region
Maritime boundaries see KZA1430+
Space (Airspace) boundaries see KZD1420+
International waters
Class here general and comprehensive works on international status, control, etc. of rivers, straits, gulfs and bays
For their function as international waterways, i.e. highways of transportation see K4194
3686 General works
3700 Rivers, lakes and seas
For particular rivers and lakes, see the appropriate region (e. g. Europe, KJC; Middle East, KMC; South and Southeast Asia, and East Asia, KNC; etc.)
For legal regimes of enclosed or semi-enclosed seas see KZA1686+
Canals. Interoceanic canals
Cf. HE528+ Transportation and communications
3710 General works
Panama Canal
For traffic and tolls see HE537+
For diplomacy see JZ3715+
For construction and maintenance see TC774+
3712.2 Treaties and other international agreements. Conventions. By date of signature
Subarrange each by Table K5
e. g. Clayton-Bolwer Treaty, 1850; Hay-Pauncefote Treaties, 1901-1902; Panama Canal Treaties, 1977
3715 General works
3720 Nicaragua Canal

KZ

Objects of the law of nations
Territory and its different parts
International waters
Canals. Interoceanic canals -- Continued
3730 Suez Canal
3740 Donau Canal
3750.A-Z Other interoceanic canals, A-Z
Straits
Class here works on the linkages between oceans and seas
3760 General works
Particular straits
3780 Black Sea Straits. Bosphorus and Dardanelles
3810 Baltic Straits
Including Skagerrak, Dattegat, and the Sound
3825 Strait of Dover
3835 Epirus (Greece and Albania)
3845 Strait of Gibraltar
3855 Magellan Straits
3865 Strait of Malacca
Including Singapore Strait
3867 Strait of Tiran
3868 Torres Strait
Gulfs and bays
3870 General works
(3875) Particular gulfs and bays
3875.A68 Aqaba, Gulf of
see KZA1686.7
3875.P48 Persian Gulf
see KZA1690
Islands. Archipelagoes
3880 General works
3881.A-Z Particular islands, archipelagoes, etc., A-Z
Antarctica
see subclass KWX
Outer space, the moon and other celestial bodies
see subclass KZD
The international legal community and members
Class here works on history, theory, structure and function of the international society (society of states)
Including individuals, states, and intergovernmental bodies
3900 General works
Subjects of the law of nations
For indigenous peoples see K3244+
3910 General works
3920 The individual as subject of international law

The international legal community and members
Subjects of the law of nations -- Continued
3925 Corporate bodies, associations, institutions, etc. as subjects of international law
The state as subject of international law. International person
4002 General works
International personality
4010 General works
Sovereignty and recognition see KZ4041+
4012 Equality. Rank of states. Immunity
4015 Dignity
4017 Jurisdiction
Including restrictions upon territorial jurisdiction
4020 Presupposition of international personality
Including rights of international cooperation and intercourse
Succession of international persons
4024 General works
4026 With regard to political and local rights and duties
4028 Extinction of international persons
Including annexation, dismemberment (civil war), dissolution or merger of a state into one or more states, etc.
4029 Failed states
Class here works on disabled states without effective government
Cf. JZ1317.2 Warlordism
Sovereign states
4034 General works
Sovereignty. Gradations of sovereignty
Including recognition of sovereignty (International status), governments in exile, legitimacy of governments
4041 General works
4042 Exclusive territorial control. Territorial supremacy. Quidquid est in territorio, est de territorio
Doctrine of non-interference and self-help see KZ4043
4043 Means of protecting independence. Self-preservation
For treasonable propaganda endangering the state, see crimes against government in appropriate K subclasses (e. g. KJ-KKZ1 4448)
For Monroe Doctrine see JZ1482
4045 Divisibility of sovereignty
Transfer of sovereignty. State succession see KZ4024+

The international legal community and members
Subjects of the law of nations
The state as subject of international law. International person
Sovereign states
Sovereignty. Gradations of sovereignty -- Continued
4047 Loss of sovereignty
Including the state as territory under occupation
Internationalized territories see KZ3673
Suzerainty see KZ4060
Composite entities
4050 General works
4051 Condominiums
4052 Composite international persons
Including real unions. Federation (federal structure)
4053 Association of states without international personality
Including personal unions, confederations, alliances, etc.
Commonwealth of Nations
Cf. KD5020+ Law of England
4054 General works
4055 Self-governing dominions
Including British before World War I
4056 Independent states
4057 Neutralized states
4058 Revolutionary states
Semi-sovereign, dependent and vassal states
4059 General works
4060 Vassal states and suzerain states
4061 Protectorates
For a particular protectorate or country see KZ4112+
Dominions see KZ4055
Mandatory states see KZ4064
Mandates. Dependencies. Trusteeships
4063 General works
4064 Mandatory states and mandated areas. Mandate system
Trust territories. Trusteeship system
4065 General works
Trusteeship council of the UN see KZ6375
4066 Dependencies. Colonies
For works on de-colonization and national self-determination see KZ1269
4067 Mediatized states
Organs of states in conduct of international affairs and transactions
4074 General works

The international legal community and members
Subjects of the law of nations
The state as subject of international law. International person
Organs of states in conduct of international affairs and transactions -- Continued
4075 Heads of state
Departments of state. Ministries of the Exterior
4076 General works
Foreign office and foreign relations administration
see the particular jurisdiction in K subclasses
4078 Ambassadors and diplomats
Class here works on legal status, immunities, etc. of diplomats
For consular laws, codes, consular documents, etc., see the appropriate K subclasses
For diplomatic service and consular service see JZ1400+
Institution of legation
4078.3 General works
4078.5 Right of legation
Responsibility of the state
4080 General works
Government liability (Tort liability), including responsibility for the acts of organs and agents of the state see K967
4082 Responsibility to protect
4110.A-Z By region, A-Z
Including works on legal (international) status of a region or of countries in such a region collectively
Aegean islands Region see KZ4110.M44
Antarctic regions see KZ4110.P65
Arctic regions see KZ4110.P65
4110.A85 Atlantic regions
Including North Atlantic region, North Sea region, South Atlantic region
4110.I64 Indian Ocean Region
4110.M44 Mediterranean Region
Including islands, e. g. Aegean islands
Pacific region see KZ4730+
4110.P65 Polar regions
Including works on both Arctic regions, Barents Sea, and Antarctic regions
For a particular country in the regions, see the country, e. g. Norway
For Antarctica see KWX1+

The international legal community and members
Subjects of the law of nations -- Continued
By state
Including works on legal (international) status of a country (jurisdiction), including older works, in particular works previously classed in JX4084+
The Americas
4112 General works
4113 United States
4114 Canada
4115 Greenland
Latin America
4116 General works
4117 Mexico
Central America
4118 General works
4119 Belize
4120 Costa Rica
4121 Guatemala
4122 Honduras
4123 Nicaragua
4124 Panama
4125 El Salvador
West Indies. Caribbean Area
Including Federation of the West Indies, 1958-1962
4128 General works
4129 Cuba
Including Guantánamo Bay Naval Base
4130 Haiti
4131 Dominican Republic
4132 Puerto Rico
4133 Virgin Islands of the United States. Danish West Indies
4134 British West Indies
Danish West Indies see KZ4133
4136 Netherlands Antilles. Dutch West Indies
Including Curaçao
For Suriname (Dutch Guiana) see KZ4149
4137 French West Indies
Including Guadeloupe and Martinique
For French Guiana see KZ4150
South America
4140 General works
4141 Argentina
4142 Bolivia
4144 Brazil
4145 Chile

The international legal community and members
Subjects of the law of nations
By state
The Americas
Latin America
South America -- Continued

4146 Colombia
4147 Ecuador
Guiana
4148 General works
Guyana. British Guiana see KZ4134
4149 Suriname. Dutch Guiana
4150 French Guiana
4152 Paraguay
4153 Peru
4154 Uruguay
4155 Venezuela
4157 Falkland Islands
Europe
4160 General works
Great Britain
4161 General works
Class here works on England, and England, Wales, Scotland and Northern Ireland combined
4162 Wales
4163 Scotland
Gibraltar see KZ4602
4165 Northern Ireland
4166 Ireland. Eire
4168 Austria. Austro-Hungarian Monarchy
4170 Hungary
4172 Czechoslovakia (to 1993). Czech Republic
4174 Slovakia (1993-)
4176 France
4178 Monaco
4180 Germany
Including the Federal Republic of Germany (to 1992)
4181 Germany (Democratic Republic) (to 1992)
4183 Greece
4185 Italy
4187 Vatican City. Stato Pontificio
Including the Papal States, territories, regions, etc. and including the periods before the Lateran treaty of 1929
For the period after 1929 see KBU4064+
4188 Andorra
4190 San Marino

The international legal community and members
Subjects of the law of nations
By state
Europe -- Continued
4192 Malta
Benelux countries. Low countries
4194 General works
4196 Belgium
4197 The Netherlands. Holland
Including individual provinces and historic (defunct) jurisdictions
Holland see KZ4197
4198 Luxembourg
4200 Russia. Soviet Union (to 1991)
Including works on the Commonwealth of Independent States; on former Soviet Republics (collectively), and on other historic (defunct) states; etc.
4204 Russia (Federation, 1992-)
Caucasus see KZ4310+
4206 Belarus
4208 Moldova
4210 Ukraine
4212 Poland
4214 Finland
Including islands
Baltic States
4216 General works
4218 Estonia
4220 Latvia
4222 Lithuania
Scandinavia
4225 General works
4226 Denmark
For Greenland see KZ4115
4228 Iceland
4229 Norway
4230 Sweden
4232 Spain
Gibraltar see KZ4602
4234 Portugal
4236 Switzerland
4237 Liechtenstein
Southeastern Europe. Balkan States
4240 General works
Greece see KZ4183
4242 Turkey
4244 Cyprus

The international legal community and members
Subjects of the law of nations
By state
Europe
Southeastern Europe. Balkan States -- Continued
4246 Albania
4248 Bulgaria
4250 Montenegro
4252 Romania
4255 Yugoslavia (to 1992). Serbia
4257 Croatia
4259 Bosnia and Hercegovina
4261 Slovenia
4263 Macedonia (Republic)
4264 Kosovo (Republic)
Asia
4270 General works
Middle East. Southwest Asia
4272 General works
4273 Armenia (to 1921)
4275 Bahrain
Gaza see KZ4282
4278 Iran
4280 Iraq
4282 Israel. Palestine
4284 Jerusalem
4286 Jordan
West Bank (Territory under Israeli occupation, 1967-) see KZ4282
4290 Kuwait
4292 Lebanon
4294 Oman
4295 Palestine (to 1948)
4297 Qatar
4299 Saudi Arabia
Southern Yemen see KZ4309
4301 Syria
4303 United Arab Emirates
4305 Yemen
4309 Yemen (People's Democratic Republic) (to 1990)
Previously Southern Yemen
Caucasus
4310 General works
4312 Armenia (Republic)
4314 Azerbaijan
4316 Georgia (Republic)
Turkey see KZ4242

The international legal community and members
Subjects of the law of nations
By state
Asia
Middle East. Southwest Asia -- Continued
Cyprus see KZ4244
Central Asia
4320 General works
4322 Kazakhstan
4324 Kyrgyzstan
4326 Tadjikistan
4328 Turkmenistan
4330 Uzbekistan
South Asia. Southeast Asia. East Asia
4335 General works
For works on Asian and Pacific areas combined see KZ4730
4337 Afghanistan
4339 Bangladesh
4341 Bhutan
4343 Brunei
4345 Burma. Myanmar
4347 Cambodia
China (to 1949)
4350 General works
4360.A-Z Provinces, A-Z
4360.A63 An-tung sheng. Andong Sheng. 安東省
4360.C53 Ch‘a-ha-erh sheng. Chaha'er Sheng. 察哈爾省
Fukien Province. Fujian Sheng. 福建省 see KZ4378.A+
4360.H64 Ho-Chiang sheng. Hejiang Sheng. 合江省
4360.H75 Hsi-k‘ang sheng. Xikang Sheng. 西康省
4360.H76 Hsing-an sheng. Xing'an Sheng. 興安省
4360.J44 Je-ho sheng. Rehe Sheng. 熱河省
Kwangsi Province. Kuang-hsi sheng. Guangxi Sheng. 廣西省 see KZ4378.A+
Kwangtung Province. Guangdong Sheng. 廣東省 see KZ4378.A+
4360.L53 Liao-pei sheng. Liaobei Sheng. 遼北省
4360.M36 Manchoukuo. Manzhouguo. Manchuria. 滿洲國
4360.N46 Nen-Chiang sheng. Nenjiang Sheng. 嫩江省
4360.N56 Ning-hsia sheng. Ningxia Sheng. 寧夏省
4360.P56 Pin-Chiang sheng. Binjiang Sheng. 濱江省
Sikang Province. Xikang Sheng. 西康省 see KZ4378.A+
4360.S85 Sui-yüan sheng. Suiyuan Sheng. 綏遠省
4360.S87 Sung-Chiang sheng. Songjiang Sheng. 松江省

The international legal community and members
Subjects of the law of nations
By state
Asia
South Asia. Southeast Asia. East Asia
China (to 1949)
Provinces, A-Z -- Continued
4360.T35 T'ai-wan sheng. Taiwan Sheng. 臺灣省
4372 China (Republic, 1949-). Taiwan
China (Peoples Republic, 1949-)
4376 General works
4378.A-Z Provinces, autonomous regions and municipalities, A-Z
4378.H66 Hong Kong
4378.T55 Tibet
4390 Timor-Leste. East Timor
India
4400 General works
States, Union Territories, etc.
4402 Andaman and Nicobar Islands
4404 Andrah Pradesh
4405 Arunchal Pradesh
4407 Assam
4409 Bihar
4411 Calcutta/Bengal Presidency
4413 Chandighar
4415 Dadra and Nagar Haveli
4417 Delhi
4419 Goa, Daman, and Diu
4421 Gujarat
4423 Haryana
4425 Himachal Pradesh
4425.5 Hyderabad
4428 Jaipur
4430 Jammu and Kashmir
4432 Karnataka
4435 Kerala
4436 Kumaon
4437 Lakshadweep
4439 Madhya Pradesh
4441 Madras Presidency
4443 Maharashtra
4445 Manipur
4447 Meghalaya
4449 Mizoram
Mysore see KZ4467
4451 Nagaland

The international legal community and members
Subjects of the law of nations
By state
Asia
South Asia. Southeast Asia. East Asia
India
States, Union Territories, etc. -- Continued

4453 Orissa
4455 Pondicherry
4457 Punjab
4459 Rajasthan
4461 Sikkim
4463 Tamil Nadu
4465 Tripura
4467 Uttar Pradesh
4469 West Bengal
4475 French Indochina
Indonesia
4477 General works
4477.5.A-Z Provinces, A-Z
<4477.5.T56> Timor Timur
see KZ4390
4479 Japan
4483 South Korea
4486 North Korea
4488 Korea (to 1945)
4490 Laos
4492 Macau
Malaysia
4494 General works
4495.A-Z Individual states, A-Z
4495.F44 Federated Malay States (1896-1942)
4495.M35 Malaya (1948-1962)
4495.M36 Malayan Union (1946-1947)
4495.S87 Straits Settlements (to 1942)
States of East and West Malaysia (1957-)
Brunei see KZ4343
4496 Federal Territory (Kuala Lumpur)
4496.5 Johor
4497 Kedah
4497.5 Kelantan
4498 Malacca
4498.5 Negeri Sembilan
4499 Pahang
4499.5 Pinang
4500 Perak
4500.5 Perlis

The international legal community and members
Subjects of the law of nations
By state
Asia
South Asia. Southeast Asia. East Asia
Malaysia
States of East and West Malaysia (1957-) -- Continued
4501 Sabah
Previously North Borneo
4501.5 Sarawak
4502 Selangor
4503 Terengganu
4504 Labuan
4506 Maldives
4507 Mongolia
Myanmar see KZ4345
4509 Nepal
4511 Pakistan
4513 Philippines
4515 Singapore
4518 Sri Lanka. Ceylon
4520 Thailand
4525 Vietnam (1976-)
Including the periods up through 1945
4528 Vietnam (Republic). South Vietnam (1946-1975)
4530 Vietnam (Democratic Republic). North Vietnam (1946-1975)
Africa
4540 General works
4542 Algeria
4544 Angola
4546 Benin
4550 Botswana
4552 British Central Africa Protectorate
4555 British Indian Ocean Territory
4556 British Somaliland
4560 Burkina Faso
4562 Burundi
4565 Cameroon
4567 Cape Verde
4569 Central African Republic
4573 Chad
4576 Comoros
4580 Congo (Brazzaville)
Congo (Democratic Republic) see KZ4716
4582 Côte d'Ivoire. Ivory Coast

The international legal community and members
Subjects of the law of nations
By state
Africa -- Continued

4584 Djibouti
4586 East Africa Protectorate
4588 Egypt
4589 Eritrea
4590 Ethiopia
4592 French Equatorial Africa
4593 French West Africa
4595 Gabon
4597 Gambia
4599 German East Africa
4600 Ghana
4602 Gibraltar
4604 Guinea
4606 Guinea-Bissau
4608 Equatorial Guinea
4610 Ifni
4612 Italian East Africa
4614 Italian Somaliland
4616 Kenya
4618 Lesotho
4620 Liberia
4622 Libya
4624 Madagascar
4626 Malawi
4628 Mali
4630 Mauritania
4633 Mauritius
4635 Mayotte
4637 Morocco
4639 Mozambique
4643 Namibia
4645 Niger
4650 Nigeria
4653 Réunion
4655 Rwanda
4657 Saint Helena
4660 Sao Tome and Principe
4664 Senegal
4666 Seychelles
4668 Sierra Leone
4670 Somalia
South Africa, Republic of
4680 General works

The international legal community and members
Subjects of the law of nations
By state
Africa
South Africa, Republic of -- Continued

4682.A-Z Provinces and self-governing territories, A-Z
Including former independent homelands
4682.B66 Bophuthatswana
4682.C36 Cape of Good Hope. Kaapland (to 1994)
4682.C57 Ciskei
4682.E36 Eastern Cape
Eastern Transvaal see KZ4682.M68
4682.F74 Free State. Orange Free State
4682.G38 Gauteng
4682.K93 KwaZulu-Natal. Natal
Including former KwaZulu Homeland areas
4682.M68 Mpulamanga. Eastern Transvaal
Natal see KZ4682.K93
4682.N64 North West
4682.N65 Northern Cape
4682.N67 Northern Province. Northern Transvaal
Northern Transvaal see KZ4682.N67
Orange Free State. Oranje Vrystaat see KZ4682.F74
4682.T73 Transkei
4682.T74 Transvaal
4682.V46 Venda
4682.W47 Western Cape
4700 Spanish West Africa (to 1958)
4702 Spanish Sahara (to 1975)
4704 Sudan
4706 Swaziland
4708 Tanzania
4710 Togo
4712 Tunisia
4714 Uganda
4716 Congo (Democratic Republic). Zaïre
4720 Zambia
4722 Zanzibar (to 1964)
4724 Zimbabwe
Pacific Area
4730 General works
Including works on both Pacific and Asian areas combined
Australia
4735 General works
States and territories

KZ

The international legal community and members
Subjects of the law of nations
By state
Pacific Area
Australia
States and territories -- Continued

4738 Australian Capital Territory
4740 Northern Territory
4742 New South Wales
4744 Queensland
4746 South Australia
4748 Tasmania
4750 Victoria
4752 Western Australia
External territories
4754 Norfolk Island
Australian Antarctic Territory see KWX125
New Zealand
4760 General works
4760.5.A-Z Regions and overseas territories, A-Z
Ross Dependency see KWX185
Other Pacific Area jurisdictions
4770 American Samoa
4772 British New Guinea (Territory of Papua)
4774 Cook Islands
4776 Easter Island
4778 Fiji
4780 French Polynesia
4782 German New Guinea (to 1914)
4784 Guam
4788 Kiribati
4790 Marshall Islands
4792 Micronesia (Federated States)
4794 Midway Islands
4796 Nauru
4798 Netherlands New Guinea (to 1963)
4800 New Caledonia
4802 Niue
4803 Northern Mariana Islands
4804 Pacific Islands (Trust Territory)
4805 Palau
4806 Papua New Guinea
4807 Pitcairn Island
4808 Solomon Islands
4810 Tonga
4812 Tuvalu
4814 Vanuatu

The international legal community and members
Subjects of the law of nations
By state
Pacific Area
Other Pacific Area jurisdictions -- Continued
4816 Wake Islands
4818 Wallis and Futuna Islands
4820 Samoa. Western Samoa
4825 Developing countries
Antarctica see KWX1+
<4835-4848> International non-governmental organizations. NGOs
see JZ4835+
Intergovernmental organizations. IGOs
4850 General works
Universal organizations
4852 General works
International unions and specialized international agencies limited in their jurisdiction by mandate
see the subject, e. g. International Labor Organization, HD7801; Universal Postal Union, K4247+; International Monetary Fund, K4452; etc.
Bodies and specialized agencies of the League of Nations and United Nations limited by mandate
see the subject
The League of Nations. Societé des nations
Bibliography
Including indexes, registers, and other finding aids
4853 General
Including the organs of the League, international unions, and specialized agencies under direction of the League
By subject
see the subject
4860 Periodicals
4860.3 Annuals. Yearbooks
For yearbooks by specialization, see the subject
4860.5 Official Journal

The international legal community and members
Subjects of the law of nations
Intergovernmental organizations. IGOs
Universal organizations
The League of Nations. Societé des nations -- Continued

4861 Intergovernmental congresses and conferences. League of Nations conferences. By name of the congress or conference

For intergovernmental congresses limited in their jurisdiction by subject, see the subject, e. g. Conferences for the Reduction and Limitation of Armaments, KZ5615+; Conference for the Codification of International Law, The Hague, 1930, KZ1287; etc.

For the preliminary congresses related to the establishment of the League see KZ4873.A+

Official acts

4862 Indexes and tables. Digests

4863 Collections. Compilations

Treaties and other international agreements. Conventions

Class here treaties concluded by the League

4863.5 Indexes and tables. Registers

Collections. Compilations

Including either multilateral or bilateral treaties, or both, and related agreements (supplemental and amendatory agreements, protocols, etc.)

4865 Serials

For League of Nations Treaty Series see KZ170+

4865.3 Monographs. By date

Individual treaties

see the subject, e. g. Convention for the Prevention and Punishment of Terrorism, 1937

Rules and regulations. Internal statutes

4865.5 Indexes and tables. Digests

4865.7 Collections

Indivdual

see the issuing organ, agency, or subject

4866 Declarations. Resolutions. Interim agreements, etc.

4867 Official reports and related materials

Including reports of advisory groups of experts

For official reports, memoranda, etc. of a particular organ, agency, bureau, etc., see the issuing organ, agency, bureau, etc.

The international legal community and members
Subjects of the law of nations
Intergovernmental organizations. IGOs
Universal organizations
The League of Nations. Societé des nations -- Continued

<4868> Dictionaries. Thesauri
see JZ4868

<4869> Handbooks. Manuals. Reference aids
see JZ4869

<4869.3> Form books, graphic materials, etc.
see JZ4871

<4870.2> Directories
see JZ4870+

4870.5.A-Z Societies. Associations. Academies, etc. By name, A-Z

4870.7 Conferences. Symposia

4871 General works
Including compends, essays, festschriften, etc.

4871.3.A-Z Manuals and other works for particular groups of users. By user, A-Z

Organization law. Constitution of the League of Nations

4873.A-Z Intergovernmental congresses and conferences. By name of the congress, A-Z
Under each:
.xA12-.xA199 Serials
.xA3 Monographs. By date
Including preliminary congresses related to the establishment of the League

Agreements, declarations, and resolutions relating to the establishment and expansion of the League of Nations

4874 Indexes and tables

4875 Collections. Selections

4876 Proposed agreements and declarations. By date

Individual agreements and declarations establishing and expanding the League of Nations

The Covenant of the League of Nations

4877.3.A12 Official drafts. By date of publication

4877.3.A2 Texts. Unannotated and annotated editions. By date of publication
Including official editions with or without annotation

The international legal community and members
Subjects of the law of nations
Intergovernmental organizations. IGOs
Universal organizations
The League of Nations. Societé des nations
Organization law. Constitution of the League of Nations
Agreements, declarations, and resolutions relating to the establishment and expansion of the League of Nations
Individual agreements and declarations establishing and expanding the League of Nations
The Covenant of the League of Nations -- Continued

4877.3.A3-.Z39 Annotated editions. Commentaries. Works on the Covenant
Including (contemporary) criticism, private drafts, etc.

Related agreements
Including supplementary bilateral agreements, and amendments, protocols, etc.
For proposed amendments see KZ4876

4877.3.Z4 Collections. Selections

4877.3.Z5 Individual agreements. By date of signature

4877.3.Z6 Indexes and tables

Miscellaneous documents of advisory commissions. Reports on application of the Covenant see KZ4875

Works on the Covenant see KZ4877.3.A3+

4877.4 Other agreements. By date of signature

Sources and relationships of the law

4878 Treaties and agreements concluded by member nations
For registration with the Secretariat of the League see KZ170

4879 Constitutional aspects of international cooperation and of membership in other international organizations

Intra-organizational (Internal) relations. The League and member nations

4880 Sovereignty question. Right of legation

4881 Rule of law

4882 Cooperation of the states

4883 Admission of new member states. Termination of membership and expulsion

The international legal community and members
Subjects of the law of nations
Intergovernmental organizations. IGOs
Universal organizations
The League of Nations. Societé des nations
Organization law. Constitution of the League of Nations -- Continued
Foreign (External) relations. International cooperation
4884 Treaty-making power
For international agreements on a particular subject, see the subject
4885 Relations with non-member states
4886 Election law
Including elections to particular offices
Organs and institutions of the League of Nations
Class here works on organs, organizations, and advisory commissions, etc. of the League
For documents (Core collections) see JZ4895+
4887 General works
4888 Diplomatic privileges and immunities of officials
Tort liability see K967.5
Assembly (Conference of the members of the League)
Documents see JZ4895+
4889 General works
Journal see KZ4860.5
4890 Representatives
List of delegates see JZ4870.2
4892 Rules of procedure of the Assembly
Council (Executive of the League)
Documents see JZ4910
4893 General works
Secretariat
4894 General works
4894.3 Secretary-General
4894.7 International civil service status
International unions, bureaus, and organizations, etc. under direction of the League
For organizations, institutions, international bureau under direction of the League, etc. with jurisdiction limited by subject, see the subject
For documents see JZ4920+
International Institute for the Unification of Private Law see K614+
International Institute of Intellectual Co-operation see K1401+

The international legal community and members
Subjects of the law of nations
Intergovernmental organizations. IGOs
Universal organizations
The League of Nations. Societé des nations
Organization law. Constitution of the League of Nations
International unions, bureaus, and organizations, etc. under direction of the League -- Continued
International Commission for Air Navigation
see subclass K
Bureau international d'assistance
see subclass K
International Relief Union
see subclass K
Nansen International Office for Refugees
see subclass K

<4895-4934> League of Nations documents and publications (Core Collection)
see JZ4895+

The United Nations. Nations unies. UN. ONU
Bibliography

<4935-4944> General bibliography
Including indexes, registers and other finding aids
Covering all UN bodies
see JZ4935+

<4935> Serials
see JZ4935+

<4936> Monographs
see JZ4936+

By UN organ, UN body or program
see the organ, body or program

By subject
see the subject, e. g. bibliography on the law of the sea, see KZA1002; human rights bibliography, see K3236; etc.

<4945> Periodicals
see JZ4945

Annuals. Yearbooks
For yearbooks by specialization, see the subject, e. g. Yearbook of Human Rights

<4947> Yearbook of the United Nations
see JZ4947

4949 United Nations Juridical Yearbook

United Nations International Law Commission Yearbook see KZ21

The international legal community and members
Subjects of the law of nations
Intergovernmental organizations. IGOs
Universal organizations
The United Nations. Nations unies. UN. ONU -- Continued
United Nations documents and publications (Core collection) see JZ5010+
4952 Monographic series (numbered)
For UN Conferences see JZ5090+
For the preliminary congresses related to the establishment of the UN see KZ4988+
4954.A-Z Intergovernmental congresses and conferences. By name of the congress, A-Z
Under each:
.xA12-.xA199 Serials
.xA13 Monographs. By date
Including ad hoc conferences of heads of state, and including proceedings, reports, resolutions, final acts, and works on the congress
For intergovernmental congresses on a particular subject, see the subject
Non-governmental congresses and conferences see KZ4984
Official acts
4956 Indexes and tables. Digests
4957 Collections. Compilations
Treaties and other international agreements. Conventions
For individual treaties, see the subject
For the Treaty Series see KZ172
For treaties and agreements (individual or collected) establishing the UN, or supplementary and ammendatory agreements see KZ4989+
Rules and regulations. Internal statutes
4962 Indexes and tables. Digests
Collections
4963 Serials
4964 Monographs. By date
Individual
see the particular organ, agency, or subject
Resolutions and decisions adopted by the general assembly. Interim arrangements, etc.
Collections (General)
see JZ5010+ Suppl. 47, 51, 53, etc.

KZ

The international legal community and members
Subjects of the law of nations
Intergovernmental organizations. IGOs
Universal organizations
The United Nations. Nations unies. UN. ONU
Official acts
Resolutions and decisions adopted by the general assembly. Interim arrangements, etc. -- Continued
Individual
see the particular organ, body, committee, or subject
Official reports
Including reports of advisory groups of experts
see JZ5010+ Supplements no. 1-53
4968 Encyclopedias
e. g. Encyclopedia of the United Nations and International Agreements
<4969> Dictionaries. Thesauri
see JZ4969
<4970-4976> Handbooks. Reference aids
see JZ4970+
<4978> Form books. Graphic materials
see JZ4978
<4979-4982> Directories
see JZ4979+
4983.A-Z Societies. Associations. Academies, etc. By name, A-Z
Academic Council on the United Nations System. ACUNS see JZ4983.A33
United Nations Association for the United States see JZ4983.U65
4984 Conferences. Symposia
<4984.5> General works
see KZ4986
The United Nations System. Organization law. Constitution of the UN
4985 Bibliography
4986 General works
Intergovernmental congresses and conferences related to the establishment of the UN. By name of the congress
Cf. JZ4988 International relations
Dumbarton Oaks Conference, 1944
4988 Serials
4988.2 Monographs. By date

The international legal community and members
Subjects of the law of nations
Intergovernmental organizations. IGOs
Universal organizations
The United Nations. Nations unies. UN. ONU
The United Nations System. Organization law.
Constitution of the UN
Intergovernmental congresses and conferences related to the establishment of the UN. By name of the congress -- Continued

4988.5 United Nations Conference on International Organization. San Francisco Conference, 1945

Including comments and proposed amendments concerning the Dumbarton Oaks proposal, 1945, and documents of the United Nations Conference on International Organization, 1945

Agreements. Declarations, and resolutions relating to the establishment of the United Nations. GENESIS

4989 Indexes and tables. Digests

4989.5 Collections. Selections

4990 Proposed agreements, declarations, etc. By date

4990.2 Individual declarations and agreements predating the establishing of the UN. By date of signature

e. g.

Declaration of London, 1941 (Resolution of the Governments engaged in the Fight Against Agression)

Atlantic Charter, 1941 (signed by President Franklin D. Roosevelt and Prime Minister Churchill)

Declaration by United Nations, 1942

Declaration of Moscow by Four Nations, 1943

Declaration of Teheran, 1943 (Declaration of the Three Powers)

Charter of the United Nations, 1945. Basic law

4991.A12 Official drafts. By date

e. g.

Dumbarton Oaks Proposal, 1944

San Francisco Draft, 1945

Private proposals and drafts see KZ4991.A3+

4991.A2 Texts. Unannotated editions. By date

The international legal community and members
Subjects of the law of nations
Intergovernmental organizations. IGOs
Universal organizations
The United Nations. Nations unies. UN. ONU
The United Nations System. Organization law.
Constitution of the UN
Charter of the United Nations, 1945. Basic law -- Continued

4991.A3-.Z39 Annotated editions. Commentaries. Works on the charter
Including (contemporary) criticism, private drafts, etc.

Related agreements
Including supplementary bilateral agreements, and amendments, protocols, etc.

4991.Z4 Collections. Selections. By date

4991.Z5 Individual agreements. By date of signature
e. g.
First Supplemental agreement regarding the Headquarters of the UN, 1966
Second Supplemental agreement regarding the Headquarters of the UN, 1969

4991.Z6 Indexes and tables

Miscellaneous documents of advisory or research commissions, etc. see KZ4989.5

Works on the agreement see KZ4991.A3+

Constitutional principles

4992 Rule of law

4992.2 Lawmaking (rulemaking) power. Treaty-making power
For enforcement mechanisms and techniques see KZ6376

Sovereignty questions, equality of member states, and immunity of member states see KZ4998+

Immunity of UN organs
see the organ

Expansion of the UN see KZ4997+

Source of the law. United Nations law making and cooperation

4992.7 Treaties and agreements

International cooperation
Including comparative organizational law

4993 General works

Relationship of the UN and its organs to other intergovernmental organizations, including regional organizations see KZ5003.A+

The international legal community and members
Subjects of the law of nations
Intergovernmental organizations. IGOs
Universal organizations
The United Nations. Nations unies. UN. ONU
The United Nations System. Organization law. Constitution of the UN
Source of the law. United Nations law making and cooperation
International cooperation -- Continued
Relationship of the UN and its organs to non-governmental organizations see KZ5003.A+
Intra-organizational (internal) relations
Including member nations, observers, and relations to its specialized agencies
4995 General works
Membership
For lists of member nations see JZ4980
4996 General works
Expansion of membership. Termination of membership. Legal problems
4997 General works
4997.5.A-Z UN relations with member nations, A-Z
Sovereignty questions
Including immunity of member nations
4998 General works
4998.5 Jurisdiction. Domestic jurisdiction
4998.7 Status of observers
Including non-member nations, IGOs and other organizations
4999 Seat of the UN Headquarters and other UN offices
Including Geneva and Vienna offices
4999.5 Rules governing the official languages of the UN
Foreign (external) relations
5000 General works
Treaty making power and practice see KZ4992.2
5001 Political cooperation of Foreign Ministers
5002.A-Z Relation with non-member nations, A-Z
5003.A-Z Relation with IGOs and other international organizations, A-Z
5004 Election law
Including election to particular offices
Responsibility and tort liability of international agencies and their organs see K967.5

The international legal community and members
Subjects of the law of nations
Intergovernmental organizations. IGOs
Universal organizations
The United Nations. Nations unies. UN. ONU
The United Nations System. Organization law.
Constitution of the UN -- Continued
UN organs, bodies and programs
For organs, specialized agencies, etc. with jurisdiction limited by mandate (subject), see the subject

5005 Bibliography

5005.2 General works
Cf. JZ5005 International relations

General Assembly
Including procedural/sessional committees and standing/inter-sessional and ad-hoc committees, and including works on subsidiary and treaty bodies collectively

5006 Bibliography

5006.2 General works
Including privately published collections of resolutions, reports, etc.
Cf. JZ5006.A+ International relations

<5010> Documents and publications (Core collection)
see JZ5010.2+

5012 President. Vice president

5013 Powers and duties
Including legislative functions and process, and immunity

General Assembly subsidiary, ad-hoc and treaty bodies

<5020> Documents and publications (Core collections)
see JZ5020 and JZ5010+ Supplements

General works see KZ5005.2

Particular bodies, committees, etc. limited in jurisdiction by mandate (subject)
see the subject, e. g. Administrative Tribunal, see KZ5274; Conferences on Disarmament, 1978- , see KZ5615+; United Nations Commission on Human Rights, see K3241; Committee on the Rights of the Child, see K639

Security Council
Including works on committees and other bodies collectively

The international legal community and members
Subjects of the law of nations
Intergovernmental organizations. IGOs
Universal organizations
The United Nations. Nations unies. UN. ONU
The United Nations System. Organization law.
Constitution of the UN
UN organs, bodies and programs
Security Council -- Continued

<5030-5035> Official records. SCOR (Core collections)
see JZ5030+
5036 General works
5037 Permanent and nonpermanent membership
5038 Powers and duties. Immunities
Peacekeeping forces and missions see KZ6376
Atomic Energy Commission
<5040-5043> Documents and publications, 1946-1952 (Core collection)
see JZ5040+
5044 General works
Disarmament Commission
<5045-5048> Official records. DCOR, 1952-1959 (Core collections)
see JZ5045+
5049 General works
Economic and Social Council
Including works on committees and other bodies collectively
5056 General works
5057 President
5057.5 Membership
Functional commissions. Standing committees, expert and other related bodies
For commissions and subsidiary bodies limited in jurisdiction by region and/or mandate (subject), see the region and/or mandate (subject)
Official records. Documentation (Core collection) see JZ5050
General works see KZ5056
5058.A-Z By commission, standing committee, etc., A-Z
Trusteeship Council. Conseil de tutelle
<5060-5065> Trusteeship Council official records. TCOR. Documentation
see JZ5060+
5066 General works
5067 President

The international legal community and members
Subjects of the law of nations
Intergovernmental organizations. IGOs
Universal organizations
The United Nations. Nations unies. UN. ONU
The United Nations System. Organization law.
Constitution of the UN
UN organs, bodies and programs
Trusteeship Council. Conseil de tutelle
Trusteeship Council official records. TCOR.
Documentation -- Continued
5068 Membership
5069 Powers and duties
Trade and Development Board. TDB
<5070-5075> Trade and Development Board official records. TDBOR (Core collection)
see JZ5070+
5076 General works
Meeting of States Parties on Human Rights Treaties
<5080-5083> Documents and publications (Core collection)
see JZ5080+
5084 General works
Secretariat
5085 General works
5086 Secretary-General. Executive Office of the Secretary-General (Chef de Cabinet)
Undersecretaries-General
5087 General works
5087.5 By specialization
Assistant Secretaries-General
5088 General works
5089 By specialization. Specialized agencies
For United Nations High Commissioner for Human Rights see K3236+
International Court of Justice (ICJ) see KZ6272+
International Criminal Court (2002 -) see KZ7250+
<5090-5197> UN sales publications and working documents
see JZ5090+
General Agreement on Tariffis and Trade. GATT
From January 1, 1995, World Trade Organization. WTO
<5185> Official records
see JZ5185
General works see K4609.5
International Civil Aviation Organization. ICAO

The international legal community and members
Subjects of the law of nations
Intergovernmental organizations. IGOs
Universal organizations
The United Nations. Nations unies. UN. ONU
Other UN bodies and programs
International Civil Aviation Organization. ICAO -- Continued
<5195> Official records
see JZ5195
General works see K4097
International Labour Organisation. ILO
<5200> Official records
see JZ5200
General works see HD7801
World Health Organization. WHO
<5230> Official records
see JZ5230
General works see RA8.A+
International Civil Service
Including the International Civil Service Commission, officials and employees
For the official report of the International Civil Service Commission, see JZ5010+ Suppl. 30
5270 General works
5270.5 Incompatibility of offices
5271 Privileges and immunities of international officials and employees
5272 Appointment. Conditions of employment
Including discipline, remuneration, allowances, etc.
Retirement
5273 General works
5273.5 Joint Staff Pension Board
5274 Administrative Tribunal
5274.5 Finance. Budget
For the financial reports and audited financial statements, see JZ5010+ Suppl. 5-7, 43, 49, etc.
5275 Postal administration
Other intergovernmental organizations
For organizations limited in jurisdiciton by mandate (subject), see the subject
For Universal Postal Union, see K4247+; World Intellectual Property Organization, see K1403+; International Maritime Organization (IMO), see K4150.2; International Monetary Fund (IMF), see K4452; International Telecommuinication Union, see K4306

The international legal community and members
Subjects of the law of nations
Intergovernmental organizations. IGOs
Universal organizations
Other intergovernmental organizations -- Continued
5280 Organisation internationale de la francophonie
Regional organizations
For international organizations limited in jurisdiction by region and/or mandate (subject), see the region and/or subject
<5330> Regionalism
see KZ1273
The Americas
Including North, Central and Latin America
General
see KDZ785
Organization of American States. Organization de los Estados Americanos. OEA. OAS
<5340> Official records
see JZ5340
Commission of the Cartegena Agreement. Andean Group
<5360> Official records
see JZ5360
General
see KG736.A5
Latin American Integration Association
<5370> Official records
see JZ5370
General
see KG736.L38
Caribbean Community. CARICOM
<5375> Official records
see JZ5375
General
see KG736.C39
Central American Common Market. CACM
<5380> Official records
see JZ5380
General
see KG736.C4
Inter-American Research and Documentation Center on Vocational Training (CINTERFOR)
<5390> Official records
see JZ5390
General
see subclass KDZ

The international legal community and members
Subjects of the law of nations
Intergovernmental organizations. IGOs
Regional organizations -- Continued
Europe
General works see KJE10
Benelux Economic Union see KJE501+
Council of Europe
<5400> Official records
see JZ5400
General see KJE101+
Organization for Security and Cooperation in Europe
<5420> Official records
see JZ5420
General works see KZ6030
European Union. European Community. EC. EU
<5425> Official records
see JZ5425
General see KJE901+
European Free Trade Association. EFTA see KJE551+
European Economic Area see KJE601+
European Payment Union see KJE301+
European Fund see KJE351+
Nordic Council see KJC548
Western European Union. WEU
<5448> Official records
see JZ5448
General see KJE51+
Asia. South Asia, Southeast and East Asia
General see KNE10
Pacific Economic Cooperation Council. PEEC see KVE401+
Asia Pacific Economic Cooperation (APEC) see KVE601+
Economic and Social Commission for Asia and the Pacific. ESCAP see KVE301+
COLOMBO Plan see KNE351+
Africa
General see KQE10
East African Community. Communauté de l'Afrique de l'Est
<5456> Official records
see JZ5456
General see KQE200+

The international legal community and members
Subjects of the law of nations
Intergovernmental organizations. IGOs
Regional organizations
Africa -- Continued
Economic Community of Central African States. Communauté Economique des Etats de l'Afrique Centrale
<5458> Official records
see JZ5458
General see KQE251+
Economic Community of West African States. Communauté Economique de l'Afrique Occidental
<5459> Official records
see JZ5459
General see KQE300+
African Union. Union Africaine (2001-)
Previously Organization of African Unity (Organisation de l'Unité Africaine; OAU)(to 2001)
<5460> Official records
see JZ5460
General see KQE701+
Arab organizations
General see KME10; KQE10
Arab Common Market. Sūq al-'Arabīyah al-Mushtarakah
<5468> Official records
see JZ5468
General see KME451+
Arab Maghreb Union. AMU
<5473> Official records
see JZ5473
General see KQE1201+
Council for Arab Economic Unity. Majlis al-Wahdah al-Iqtis adiyah al-'Arabiyah
<5475> Official records
see JZ5475
General see KME151+
League of Arab States. Majlis al-Wahdah al-Iqtis adiyah al-'Arabiyah
<5480> Official records
see JZ5480
General see KME51+
Pacific Area organizations
General works see KVE10
Association of South East Asian Nations. ASEAN

The international legal community and members
Subjects of the law of nations
Intergovernmental organizations. IGOs
Regional organizations
Pacific Area organizations
Association of South East Asian Nations. ASEAN -- Continued

<5490> Official records. Documentation
see JZ5490

General works see KNE151+

Other international organizations limited in jurisdiction by mandate
see the subject, e. g. International Commission for the North West Atlantic Fisheries, see K3898; North Atlantic Treaty Organization. NATO, see KZ5925.2+; etc.

International law of peace and peace enforcement
Class here works on the legal regime of international security and prevention of war
Including history

5510 Bibliography

5511 Periodicals

5513 Monographic series (numbered)

Societies. Associations. Institutes. Academies, etc. for peace promotion, research and education

<5514-5526> General
see JZ5514+

<5518.A-Z> International associations. By name, A-Z

National associations

<5520> Carnegie Endowment for International Peace

<5520.5.A-Z> Individual chapters or divisions, A-Z

5520.5.D585 Division of international law

5528.A-Z Intergovernmental congresses and conferences. By name of the congress, A-Z
Under each:

.xA12-.xA199	*Serials*
.xA3	*Monographs. By date*

The Hague International Peace Conference, 1899 see KZ6015+

The Hague International Peace Conference, 1907 see KZ6020+

Conferences on Limitation of Armament see KZ5615.C63

5533 Encyclopedias. Dictionaries

<5534> Peace research and education
see JZ5534

5538 General works

<5544-5573> History and theory of pacifism
see JZ5544+

International law of peace and peace enforcement -- Continued

<5574-5580> Peace movements. Anti-war movements
- see JZ5574+

<5581> Peace ethics
- see JZ5581

The system of collective security

5586 Bibliography

<5587> Annuals. Yearbooks
- see JZ5587

5588 General works

5589 Types of international agreements and contracts
- Including non-aggression pacts; pacts and contracts of neutrality and territorial integrity, etc.

Renunciation and outlawry of war

5593.2 Treaties and other international agreements. By date of signature
- Subarrange each by Table K5
- e. g. General Treaty for the Renunciation of War (Pact of Paris, Kellogg-Briand Pact), 1928

5594 General works

<5595-5603> International tension and conflicts. The cold war
- see JZ5595+

By region

Latin America

Treaties and other international agreements. Conventions

5604 General (Collective)

5604.3 Multilateral treaties and conventions. By date of signature
- Subarrange each by Table K5

5604.5 General works

Europe

Treaties and other international agreements. Conventions

5605 General (Collective)

5606 Multilateral treaties and conventions. By date of signature
- Subarrange each by Table K5

5606.3 General works

Middle East

Treaties and other international agreements. Conventions

5606.5 General (Collective)

5607 Multilateral treaties and conventions. By date of signature
- Subarrange each by Table K5

5607.5 General works

International law of peace and peace enforcement
The system of collective security
By region -- Continued
Africa
Treaties and other international agreements. Conventions
5608 General (Collective)
5609 Multilateral treaties and conventions. By date of signature
Subarrange each by Table K5
5609.3 General works
5610 South Asia
5611 Southeast Asia
5612 Central Asia
5613 South Pacific
5613.5 Indian Ocean
5614 Antarctica. Antarctic Ocean
Arms control and disarmament regimes. Limitation on use and ban of weapons
Including control and limitation of manufacture, testing, and possession
Cf. UA12.5 Disarmament inspection
Bibliography see KZ5586
Annuals. Yearbooks see JZ5587
5615.A-Z Intergovernmental congresses and conferences. By name of congress, A-Z
Under each:
.xA12-.xA199 Serials
.xA3 Monographs. By date
Including standing (serial) conferences and ad hoc conferences
5615.C45 Conference for the Discontinuance of Nuclear Weapon Tests, Geneva, 1958-1962
5615.C47 Conference for the Limitation of Naval Armament, Geneva, 1927
5615.C52 Conference for the Reduction and Limitation of Armaments, Geneva, 1932-1934
5615.C55 Conference on Disarmament
Previously Committee on Disarmament (1979-1983)
5615.C58 Conference on Problems and perspectives of Conventional Disarmament in Europe, Geneva, 1989
5615.C63 Conference on the Limitation of Armament, Washington, D.C., 1921-1922
5615.I68 International Conference to Ban the Neutron Bomb, Geneva, 1978

International law of peace and peace enforcement
The system of collective security
Arms control and disarmament regimes. Limitation on use and ban of weapons
Intergovernmental congresses and conferences. By name of congress, A-Z -- Continued
5615.U55 UN International Conference (on Prohibition or Restriction of Certain Conventional Weapons), Geneva, 1979-1980
5620 Collected treaties
5624 General works
<5625-5630> International politics in arms control. Disengagement
see JZ5625+
Conventional arms control
Including mines, booby traps, incendiary weapons (napalm, flame throwers, etc.) and fragments not detectible in the human body
Intergovernmental congresses and conferences see KZ5615.A+
Treaties and other international agreements. Conventions (Multilateral)
5637 St. Petersburg Declaration, 1868 (Table K5)
5638 Hague Declaration (relative to expanding bullets), 1899 (Table K5)
5639 Hague Declaration (prohibiting of projectiles or explosives from balloons), 1899 (Table K5)
Hague Convention on Prohibition or Restrictions on the Use of Certain Conventional Weapons which may be deemed too excessively injurious or to have indiscriminate effects. Convention on Inhumane Weapons, 1981
5640.A12 Collections of miscellaneous materials. By date
Including selections of the treaty, official drafts, documents of advisory or research commissions, travaux preparatoires, etc.
5640.A15 Indexes and tables
Texts of, and works on, the treaty
5640.A2 Unannotated editions. By date
Including official editions, with or without annotations
5640.A3-.Z39 Annotated editions. Commentaries. Works on the treaty
Including private drafts

International law of peace and peace enforcement
The system of collective security
Arms control and disarmament regimes. Limitation on use and ban of weapons
Conventional arms control
Treaties and other international agreements. Conventions (Multilateral)
Hague Convention on Prohibition or Restrictions on the Use of Certain Conventional Weapons which may be deemed too excessively injurious or to have indiscriminate effects. Convention on Inhumane Weapons, 1981
Texts of, and works on, the treaty -- Continued
Related agreements
Including accessions, protocols, successions, rectifications, concessions, schedules, annexed model treaties, bilateral treaties relating to the treaty, etc.
5640.Z4 Collections. Selections
5640.Z5 Protocols. By date
e. g. Protocol (I) on Non-Detectable Fragments, The Hague 1981; Protocol (II) on Prohibition or Restriction on the use of Mines, Booby-traps and other Devices, The Hague 1981; Protocol (III) on Prohibition or Restrictions on the Use of Incendiary Weapons, The Hague 1981
Miscellaneous documents of advisory or research commissions, etc. see KZ5640.A12
Works on the treaty see KZ5640.A3+
5640.Z8 Review conferences of the parties to the treaty. By date of the conference
5642 Other treaties and conventions. By date of signature (Table K5)
5645 General works
5645.5.A-Z Particular weapons, A-Z
5645.5.C58 Cluster bombs
Weapons of mass destruction
5646 General works
Nuclear (Strategic) arms limitation, reduction, and prohibition
Intergovernmental congresses and conferences. By name of the congress
START. Strategic Arms Reduction Talks, 1982-1983
5647 Serials
5647.3 Monographs. By date

International law of peace and peace enforcement
The system of collective security
Arms control and disarmament regimes. Limitation on use and ban of weapons
Weapons of mass destruction
Nuclear (Strategic) arms limitation, reduction, and prohibition -- Continued
Treaties and other international agreements. Conventions

5649 Collections. Selections

Multilateral treaties and conventions

5650 START II. Strategic Arms Reduction Treaty, 1993 (Table K5)

5652 Other multilateral treaties and conventions. By date of signature (Table K5)

Bilateral treaties

SALT I accords between USSR and USA, 1969-1971 (Strategic Arms Limitation Talks)

Treaty on the Limitation of Anti-Ballistic Missile Systems. ABM Treaty, 1972

5660.A12 Collections of miscellaneous materials. By date

Including selections of the treaty, official drafts, documents of advisory or research commissions, travaux preparatoires, etc.

5660.A15 Indexes and tables

Texts of, and works on, the treaty

5660.A2 Unannotated editions. By date

Including official editions, with or without annotations

5660.A3-.Z39 Annotated editions. Commentaries. Works on the treaty

Including private drafts

Related agreements

Including accessions, protocols, successions, rectifications, concessions, schedules, annexed model treaties, bilateral treaties relating to the treaty, etc.

5660.Z4 Collections. Selections

5660.Z5 Protocols. By date

e. g. Protocol of 1974

Miscellaneous documents of advisory or research commissions, etc. see KZ5660.A12

Works on the treaty see KZ5660.A3+

5660.Z8 Review conferences of the parties to the treaty. By date of the conference

International law of peace and peace enforcement
The system of collective security
Arms control and disarmament regimes. Limitation on use and ban of weapons
Weapons of mass destruction
Nuclear (Strategic) arms limitation, reduction, and prohibition
Treaties and other international agreements. Conventions
Bilateral treaties
SALT I accords between USSR and USA, 1969-1971 -- Continued

5661 Interim Agreement on Certain Measures with respect to the Limitation of Strategic Offensive Arms, 1972 (Table K5)

SALT II agreements between USSR and USA, 1972-1979 (Strategic Arms Limitation Talks)

5662 Agreement on Basic Principles of Negotiations on the Further Limitation of Strategic Offensive Arms, 1973 (Table K5)

5662.2 Treaty on the Limitation of Strategic Offensive Arms, 1979 (Table K5)

5662.25 INF. Intermediate Range Nuclear Forces Treaty, 1987 (Table K5)

5662.3 START I. Strategic Arms Reduction Treaty between USA and USSR, 1991 (Table K5)

5662.32 START II. Strategic Arms Reduction Treaty between USA and Russia, 2010 (Table K5)

5663.A-Z Other treaties. By country, A-Z

Subarrange treaties of each country by date of signature. Further subarrange each treaty by Table K5

5665 General works

Nuclear nonproliferation

Including prohibition of transfer and acquisition of nuclear weapons

Treaties and other international agreements. Conventions

5670 Treaty on Non-Proliferation of Nuclear Weapons. Non-proliferation Treaty, 1968 (Table K5 modified)

5670.Z8 Review conferences. By date of conference

e. g. Review Conference of the Parties to the Treaty (1st), Geneva, 1975; Review Conference of the Parties to the Treaty (2nd), Geneva, 1980; Review Conference of the Parties to the Treaty (3rd), Geneva, 1985

International law of peace and peace enforcement
The system of collective security
Arms control and disarmament regimes. Limitation on use and ban of weapons
Weapons of mass destruction
Nuclear (Strategic) arms limitation, reduction, and prohibition
Nuclear nonproliferation -- Continued
5675 General works
Cessation of nuclear weapon tests
Treaties and other international agreements. Conventions (Multilateral)
5680 Treaty Banning Nuclear Weapon Tests in the Atmosphere, in Outer Space and under Water. Test Ban Treaty, 1963 (Table K5)
5680.2 Treaty on the Limitation of Underground Nuclear-Weapon Tests. Threshhold Test-ban Treaty, 1974 (Table K5)
5680.3 Treaty on Underground Nuclear Explosions for Peaceful Purposes. Peaceful Nuclear Explosion Treaty, 1976 (Table K5)
5680.4 Other treaties and conventions. By date of signature (Table K5)
5681 General works
5682 Nuclear weapon freeze
5684 Prohibition of the production of fissionable material for weapons purpose
Particular nuclear weapon systems
Anti-ballistic missile systems
Treaties see KZ5660+
5685 General works
5686 Neutron weapons
Nuclear weapon free zones and zones of peace
Arms control and arms limitation regimes with regard to the international commons
5687 General works
Antarctica
The Antarctic Treaty system see KWX1+
5687.5 General works
Outer Space
Treaties and other international agreements. Conventions
Treaty on Principles governing the Activities of States in Exploration and Use of Outer Space. Outer Space Treaty, 1967 see KZD1121
5690 General works

International law of peace and peace enforcement
The system of collective security
Arms control and disarmament regimes. Limitation on use and ban of weapons
Weapons of mass destruction
Nuclear weapon free zones and zones of peace
Arms control and arms limitation regimes with regard to the international commons
Outer Space -- Continued
<5695-5710> Prevention of arms race in outer space. International security dimensions
see JZ5695+
The Oceans
Including sea-bed, ocean floor and subsoil thereof
Treaties and other international agreements. Conventions
5715.2 Multilateral treaties and conventions. By date of signature
Subarrange each by Table K5
e. g. Treaty on the Prohibition of the Emplacement of Nuclear Weapons and other Weapons of Mass Destruction on the Sea-Bed and the Ocean Floor and in the Subsoil thereof, 1971
5720 General works
Establishment of nuclear-weapon-free zones
5725 General works
By region
Latin America
Treaties and other international agreements. Conventions
5730.2 Multilateral treaties and conventions. By date of signature
Subarrange each by Table K5
e. g. Treaty for the Prohibition of Nuclear Weapons in Latin America. Treaty of Tlatelolco, 1967
5735 General works
5736 Agency for the Prohibition of Nuclear Weapons in Latin America. OPANAL (1969-)
Europe
Treaties and other international agreements. Conventions
5740.2 Multilateral treaties and conventions. By date of signature
Subarrange each by Table K5

International law of peace and peace enforcement
The system of collective security
Arms control and disarmament regimes. Limitation on use and ban of weapons
Weapons of mass destruction
Nuclear weapon free zones and zones of peace
Establishment of nuclear-weapon-free zones
By region
Europe
Treaties and other international agreements. Conventions
Multilateral treaties and conventions. By date of signature -- Continued
Treaty of Rome. EURATOM Treaty, 1957
see KJE4443.31957
5745 General works
5760 Scandinavia. Northern Europe
5761 Mediterranean Region
Middle East
5765.2 Treaties and other international agreements. Conventions. By date of signature
Subarrange each by Table K5
5770 General works
Africa
Treaties and other international agreements. Conventions
5780.2 Multilateral treaties and conventions. By date of signature
Subarrange each by Table K5
e. g. Declaration on the Denuclearization of Africa, 1964
5785 General works
5786 South Asia
5786.5 Southeast Asia
5786.7 Central Asia
5787 South Pacific
5788 Indian Ocean Zone of Peace
5788.5 Antarctica. Southern Ocean
5800 Nuclear crisis control
Other weapons of mass destruction
Chemical arms control
Including chemical and biological (bacteriological) weapons, binary weapons and gases
Cf. UG447+ Military engineering
Treaties and other international agreements. Conventions
5824 Collections. Selections

International law of peace and peace enforcement
The system of collective security
Arms control and disarmament regimes. Limitation on use and ban of weapons
Weapons of mass destruction
Other weapons of mass destruction
Chemical arms control
Treaties and other international agreements. Conventions -- Continued
Multilateral treaties and conventions
5825 Hague Declaration on Asphixiating Gases, 1899 (Table K5)
5825.2 Geneva Protocol for the Prohibition of the Use in War of Asphyxiating, Poisonous or other Gases, and of Bacteriological Methods of Warfare, 1925 (Table K5)
5825.3 Geneva Convention on the Prohibition of the Development, Production, and Stockpiling of Bacteriological (Biological) and Toxin Weapons and on their Destruction, 1972 (Table K5 modified)
5825.3.Z8 Review conferences. By date of conference
e. g. First Review Conference of the Parties to the Convention, 1980; Second Review Conference of the Parties to the Convention, 1986
5826 Convention on the Prohibition of the Development, Production, Stockpiling, and use of Chemical Weapons and on their Destruction, 1993 (Table K5)
5827 Other treaties and conventions. By date of signature (Table K5)
5830 General works
5832 Chemical-weapon-free zones
Directed-energy weapons
Treaties and other international agreements. Conventions
5840.2 Multilateral treaties and conventions. By date of signature
Subarrange each by Table K5
5855 General works
5865.A-Z Other types of weapons or weapon systems, A-Z
5865.B56 Biological weapons
5865.R34 Radiological weapons
Mutual and balanced reduction of armed forces
Including post-cold war strategies of arms control
5870 Bibliography

International law of peace and peace enforcement
The system of collective security
Arms control and disarmament regimes. Limitation on use and ban of weapons
Mutual and balanced reduction of armed forces -- Continued

5872 Periodicals

5880.A-Z Intergovernmental congresses and conferences. By name of the congress, A-Z

Under each:

.xA12-.xA199	*Serials*
.xA3	*Monographs. By date*

Treaties and other international agreements. Conventions

5884 Collections. Selections

Multilateral treaties and conventions

Including regional treaties

5885 Treaty on Conventional Forces in Europe. CFE Treaty, 1992 (Table K5 modified)

5885.Z8 Review conferences. By date of conference

e. g. First Conference to Review the Operation of the Treaty on Conventional Armed Forces in Europe, 1996

5885.2 Treaty on Open Skies, 1992 (Table K5)

5886 Other treaties and conventions. By date of signature (Table K5)

5890.A-Z Bilateral treaties. By country, A-Z

Subarrange treaties of each country by date of signature. Further subarrange each treaty by Table K5

5893 General works

Military pact systems for collective self-defense

Class here the treaties and works on associated legal issues

Including both supra-regional and regional defense pacts and organizations based thereupon

For political analysis see JZ5900+

5900 General and comparative

e. g. Collective defense under the Brussels and North Atlantic treaties; United Nations and the North Atlantic Pact; Atlantic alliance and Warsaw Pact; etc.

Supra-regional

North Atlantic Treaty and North Atlantic Treaty Organization (NATO)

Treaties and other international agreements. Conventions

Multilateral treaties and conventions

North Atlantic Treaty, 1949

International law of peace and peace enforcement
Military pact systems for collective self-defense
Supra-regional
North Atlantic Treaty and North Atlantic Treaty Organization (NATO)
Treaties and other international agreements. Conventions
Multilateral treaties and conventions. By date of signature
North Atlantic Treaty, 1949 -- Continued

5925.A12 Drafts. Proposed texts. By date
5925.A15 Indexes and tables
Texts of, and works on, the treaty
5925.A2 Unannotated editions. By date
Including official editions, with or without annotations
5925.A3-.Z39 Annotated editions. Commentaries. Works on the treaty
Including private drafts
Related agreements
Including accessions, protocols, successions, rectifications, concessions, schedules, annexed model treaties, bilateral treaties relating to the treaty, etc.
5925.Z4 Collections. Selections
5925.Z5 Protocols. By date
e. g. Protocol regarding the Accession of Greece and Turkey to the North Atlantic Treaty, 1949
Works on the treaty see KZ5925.A3+
5925.Z8 Review conferences of the parties to the treaty. By date of the conference
5925.2 Bonn Convention, 1952 (Table KF7)
5930 General works
Organization
5935 North Atlantic Council
5936 Allied Command Europe
Cf. UA646.3+ Navies (Organization)
5938 Military Commission
5939 NATO Civil Defense Committee
5940.A-Z Other advisory and expert committees, panels, groups, etc. By name, A-Z
5943.A-Z Special topics, A-Z
5945 Inter-American Treaty of Reciprocal Assistance (Rio de Janeiro), 1947 (Table K5)
Regional
Europe

International law of peace and peace enforcement
Military pact systems for collective self-defense
Regional
Europe -- Continued
Brussels Treaty and Permanent Commission
5950 Treaty of Economic, Social and Cultural Collaboration and Collective Self-defense (Brussels Treaty), 1948 (Table K5)
5952 General works
5953 Brussels Treaty Permanent Commission
European Defense Community (Proposed)
5955 Draft treaty, 1952 (Table K5)
5957 General works
Warsaw Pact and Warsaw Treaty Organization
5965 Warsaw Treaty, 1955 (Table K5)
5967 General works
International police and peacekeeping forces see KZ6374+
Pacific settlement of international disputes and conflict resolution. Peace through law
For political peace literature and works on pacificism, peace movements, etc., see JZ5511.2+
6009 Bibliography
6010 General and comparative
Settlement through intergovernmental conferences and organizations
Universal. The Hague Peace system for the pacific settlement of international disputes
Individual conferences
International Peace Conference (The Hague), 1899
6015 Serials
6015.2 Monographs. By date
International Peace Conference (2nd, The Hague), 1907
6020 Serials
6020.2 Monographs. By date
6023 League of Nations conferences. By date
Under each:
.A12-.A199 *Serials*
.A3 *Monographs. By date*
6025 UN Security Council. Procedure in peaceful settlement of disputes
For document sets see JZ5030
Regional
6030 Organization for Security and Cooperation in Europe
Previously Conference on Security and Cooperation in Europe. CSCE (Organization), 1972-
Pan American Conferences

International law of peace and peace enforcement
Pacific settlement of international disputes and conflict resolution. Peace through law
Settlement through intergovernmental conferences and organizations
Regional
Pan American Conferences -- Continued
American Congress of Panama, 1826 see KZ1367
6034.A-Z International American Conferences, 1889-1948. By place, A-Z
Under each:
.xA12-.xA199 *Serials*
.xA3 *Monographs. By date*
Superseded by the Inter-American Conference, 1954- ; for the conference, see KZ6035
6034.B65 9th, Bogota, 1948
6034.M49 2nd, Mexico, 1901-1902
6035 Inter-American Conference, 1954-
Treaties and other international agreements. Conventions
Class here multilateral treaties of pacific settlement, mediation, fact finding, conciliation, etc. non-aggression, and prevention of war
For bilateral treaties, see the country
For arbitration treaties see KZ183+
6037 Collections. Selections
6038 Draft treaties. Model treaties
e. g. League of Nations. Model treaty to strengthen the means for preventing war
Individual treaties and conventions
6040 Geneva Protocol for the Pacific Settlement of International Disputes, 1924 (Table K5)
6041 Locarno Pact, 1925 (Table K5)
6042 Treaty of Paris, 1928 (General Act for Pacific Settlement of International Disputes. Kellog Pact) (Table K5)
6042.2 Inter-American Treaty on Good Offices and Mediation, 1936 (Table K5)
Inter-American Treaty of Reciprocal Assistance, 1947 see KZ5945
American Treaty of Pacific Settlement (Pact of Bogota, 1948; Charter of the OAS)
see KDZ1138
6042.3 Other treaties and conventions. By date of signature (Table K5)
Preliminary processes other than institutionalized arbitration
6044 General works

International law of peace and peace enforcement
Pacific settlement of international disputes and conflict resolution. Peace through law
Preliminary processes other than institutionalized arbitration -- Continued
6045 Mediation and good offices
For general diplomatic negotiations see JZ6045
For treaties see KZ183+
Fact finding and inquiry. International commissions of inquiry. Enquête commissions
For treaties see KZ183+
6060 General works
Particular commissions
6065 Mixed commissions under the Jay treaties (1794)
6070 Permanent international commission of inquiry under the Bryan treaties (1913/1914)
6072 Mixed commission under the German/Polish Upper Silesia Convention (1922)
Conciliation. Commission of conciliation
Treaties see KZ183+
6078 General works
6080 Association for International Conciliation
Particular commissions
6085 Conciliation Commission under the Locarno treaties (1925)
6090 Conciliation commissions under the General Act for the Pacific Settlement of International Disputes (1928 and 1949)
6095 Organization of African Unity. Commission of Mediation, Conciliation, and Arbitration
Arbitration and adjudication
6115 General works
Ius arbitrale internationale
6120 Bibliography
6124 Periodicals
6125 Annuals. Yearbooks
e. g. Annuaire de la vie internationale
Arbitration treaties see KZ183+
Arbitration cases
Universal collections see KZ200+
Cases (collected or individual) by region or country see KZ221+
Appointed arbitral tribunals
Including compulsory arbitration, and including ad hoc tribunals based on arbitration agreement (compromise); and permanent arbitral tribunals established by treaty

International law of peace and peace enforcement
Pacific settlement of international disputes and conflict resolution. Peace through law
Arbitration and adjudication
Appointed arbitral tribunals -- Continued
6144 General works
6146 Organization
Including president (umpire) and arbiters. Nomination
6148 Jurisdiction (Compulsory jurisdiction) and law applicable. Rules of international law
Including procedure and summary procedures
6158 Parties and agents
6160 Secrecy of deliberations
6162 Arbitral awards and publicity of awards
For general collections of awards see KZ200+
For awards (collected or individual) by region or country see KZ221+
Institutionalized arbitration
6165 General works
Permanent Court of Arbitration (The Hague, 1900-). Cour permanente d'arbitrage. Ständiger Schiedshof. Corte permanente di arbitrario internazionale
6170 General works
6172 Organization
Including Administrative Council and International Bureau (Registry)
6175 Jurisdiction (Compulsory jurisdiction) and Law applicable. Rules of international law
6179 Procedure and awards
Including appointment of individual tribunals under the Court's provision
6180 Validity and nullity of arbitral awards
6182 Res judicata
6183 Arbitral awards
For general collections of awards see KZ200+
For awards (collected or individual) by region or country see KZ221+
6184 Legal remedies
Including remedy in case of excess of the arbiter, recourse and revision
Enforceability. Sanctions see KZ6373
International courts
6250 General works
Permanent Court of International Justice (The Hague, 1920-1946). World Court. Cour permanente de justice internationale. PCIJ

International law of peace and peace enforcement
Pacific settlement of international disputes and conflict resolution. Peace through law
Arbitration and adjudication
International courts
Permanent Court of International Justice (The Hague, 1920-1946). World Court. Cour permanente de justice internationale. PCIJ -- Continued

6260 General works
Including history
6263 Organization. Statute. Documents
6265 Jurisdiction. Law applicable
6269 Procedure and judicial decisions
For decisions, reports see KZ206+
For pleadings see KZ210

International Court of Justice (1946-). Cour internationale de justice. ICJ
6272 Bibliography
6273 Yearbooks. Annuaire
For annual report to the UN General Assembly, see JZ5010.2 Suppl. 4
6275 General works
Including history
6277 Organization. Statute. Documents
6279 Official languages
6280 Judges. President and Vice-president
Including Registrar, and including legal status, privileges, immunities, and incompatibility
6283 Jurisdiction. Competence
Including voluntary and compulsory jurisdiction, etc.
6285 Law applicable
Including treaties and conventions, principes généraux and judicial decisions
6287 Procedure
Including official languages (English and French)
For pleadings see KZ218+
Judicial decisions
For court decisions see KZ212+
6289 General works
6290 Judgment
Including validity and nullity. Publication
6293 Res judicata
6294 Legal opinions. Interpretation and development of international law (corpus juris gentium)
Cf. KZ1284+ Methodology
Remedies
6295 General works

International law of peace and peace enforcement
Pacific settlement of international disputes and conflict resolution. Peace through law
Arbitration and adjudication
International courts
International Court of Justice (1946-). Cour internationale de justice. ICJ
Remedies -- Continued
6297 Remedies in case of excess of jurisdiction. Recourse
6299 Appellate procedure. Revision
(6304-6332) International criminal courts and tribunals
see KZ7230+
International Tribunal of the Law of the Sea see KZA5200+
Regional courts of justice
see the region (e.g. European Court of Justice. Cour de justice in subclass KJE)
Enforced settlement of international disputes. Law enforcement regimes. Law of armed conflict
6350 Bibliography
6355 General works
Non-military coercion
Including works on Drago doctrine and self-help, and including works on covert coercion
6360 General works
Reprisals. Retorsion. Retaliation (Lex talionis)
6362 General works
Particular (coercive or retaliatory) measures
6364 General works
6365 Embargo
6366 Pacific blockade. Le blocus pacifique
Intervention. Preventive intervention
Including intervention by states or intergovernmental organizations in civil wars
For preventive diplomacy and non-legal works on other preventive measures see JZ6368+
6368 General works
6369 Humanitarian intervention
<6372> Particular conflicts and crises
see KZ6795.A+
6373 Sanctions
Including economic sanctions
For works on national legislation concerning economic sanction programs, procedures, etc., see the appropriate jurisdiction in class K subclasses

Enforced settlement of international disputes. Law enforcement regimes. Law of armed conflict
Non-military coercion -- Continued
6373.2 State-sponsored targeted killing (Table KZ12)
Including works on extraterritorial counterterrorism through lethal covert operations
Threat of force. Enforced peacekeeping measures short of war
Including self-defense and use of international military force
6374 General works
6375 Under the League of Nations covenant
6376 Under the United Nations charter
Including works on UN enforcement mechanisms and enforcement techniques, e. g. verification missions
<6377.A-Z> By country providing peacekeeping forces,
see law of the country in KD - KWX
(6377.5.A-Z) Particular wars or conflicts
see KZ6795.A+
Law of war and neutrality. Jus belli
For military law see K4720+
6378 Bibliography
6379 Periodicals
6380 Monographic series
Including early works
Intergovernmental congresses and conferences
Brussels Conference, 1874
6381 Serials
6381.5 Monographs. By date
London International Naval Conference, 1908-1909 see KZ6545+
6382.A-Z Other congresses and conferences. By name of the congress, A-Z
Under each:
.xA12-.xA199 *Serials*
.xA3 *Monographs. By date*
Treaties and other international agreements. Conventions
6383 Collections. Selections
Multilateral treaties and conventions
6384 Hague Convention (V. Rights and Duties of Neutral Powers and Persons in War on Land), 1907 (Table K5)
6384.2 Hague Convention (XIII. Rights and Duties of Neutral Powers in Naval War), 1907 (Table K5)
6384.3 Hague Convention (III. Opening of Hostilities, Declaration of War, etc.), 1907 (Table K5)
Declaration of London, 1909 see KZ6554

KZ

Enforced settlement of international disputes. Law enforcement regimes. Law of armed conflict

Law of war and neutrality. Jus belli

Treaties and other international agreements. Conventions

Multilateral treaties and conventions -- Continued

6384.5 Other treaties and conventions. By date of signature (Table K5)

6385 General works

Including early treatises, e. g. Gentili, Alberico, 1552-1608, Commentationes de jure belli (1588-1589), and De jure belli, libri tres (1598)

For Grotius, Hugo, 1583-1645, De jure belli ac pacis libri tres see KZ2093.A3A+

History see KZ6385

<6390-6392> Sociology and philosophy of war

see JZ6390+

Concepts and principles

6396 Just cause and right to war. Bellum justum. Legality and illegality of war

For jihād see KBP2416

For renunciation of war see KZ5593.2+

6397 Nomenclature of war. Typology

Including civil war, guerrilla warfare, armed resistance movements, etc.

For use of coercive measures in civil wars see KZ6368+

6398.A-Z Other, A-Z

Neutralization of territory see KZ6398.R45

6398.R45 Region of war. Neutral territory

Including territory and territorial waters

Outbreak of war. Opening of hostilities. Ultimatum and declaration

Treaties and other international agreements. Conventions see KZ6384+

6399 General works

<6400> Effects on diplomacy

see JZ6340

<6401-6402> Economic aspects

see JZ6401+

6404 Effects on treaties, contracts, property, etc.

6405.A-Z Works on diverse aspects of the subject, A-Z

6405.E64 Enemy character

Including natural and juristic persons, real property, ships, goods, etc.

6405.E68 Environmental aspects

Espionage. Deception, disinformation, etc. see UB250+

6405.M47 Mercenary troops. Private military companies

Enforced settlement of international disputes. Law enforcement regimes. Law of armed conflict
Law of war and neutrality. Jus belli
Outbreak of war. Opening of hostilities. Ultimatum and declaration
Works on diverse aspects of the subject, A-Z -- Continued
6405.N66 Non-state actors
6405.N83 Nuclear facilities
Private military companies see KZ6405.M47
Belligerency. Recognition of belligerency. Belligerents
Including principles and accessories
6415 General works
6417 Alliances, succor, etc. during the state of war. Allied belligerents
6418 Armed forces and noncombatants
Neutrality
Treaties and other international agreements. Conventions
6419 Collections. Selections
6420.2 Multilateral treaties and conventions. By date of signature
Subarrange each by Table K5
Declaration of Paris, 1856 see KZ6550
Hague Convention (V. Rights and Duties of Neutral Powers and Persons in War on Land), 1907 see KZ6384
Hague Convention (XIII. Rights and Duties of Neutral Powers in Naval War), 1907 see KZ6384.2
6422 General works
6423 Different kinds of neutrality
Including armed neutrality, perpetual neutrality, voluntary and conventional neutrality, etc.
6424 Neutrality under the UN Charter
6425 Neutrality and collective measures
Including use of force and measures short of war
6425.5 Infractions of neutrality. Prohibited acts
6426 Commencement and end of neutrality
Warfare on land
Treaties and other international agreement. Conventions see KZ6384+
6427 General works

Enforced settlement of international disputes. Law enforcement regimes. Law of armed conflict
Law of war and neutrality. Jus belli
Warfare on land -- Continued
Invasion. Belligerent occupation and utilization of enemy territory. Occupatio bellica
Including economic law of occupied territories
For control of enemy property in a particular jurisdiction, see the jurisdiction (wartime and emergency legislation), e. g. KK7563 Control of enemy and alien property
For restitution, indemnification, and claims settlement, see particular jurisdictions, e. g. Germany, KK7642+
For economic aspects of occupation see JZ6401+
For occupation of enemy territory after armistice see KZ6775
6429 General works
6430 Requisitions and contributions
6432 Destruction of enemy property
6434 Control of means of transportation and communication in occupied territory
Including railway rolling stock, telecommunication, etc.
6436 Permissible violence. Devastation
6437 Bombardment and siege
Arms and instruments of war
General works
see class U
Arms control, limitation, and ban, etc. of weapons see KZ5615.A+
Humanitarian law. Usus in bello
Class here works on subjects commonly identified as "Geneva law"
Including human rights in armed conflict
For humanitarian intervention see KZ6369
6440 Bibliography
e. g. Index of International Humanitarian Law
6442 Periodicals
6443 Monographic series
Intergovernmental congresses and conferences
Conference for Revision of the Geneva Convention of 1864, Geneva, 1906
6450 Serials
6450.2 Monographs. By date
Conference for Revision of the Geneva Convention of 1906, Geneva, 1929
6452 Serials
6452.2 Monographs. By date

Enforced settlement of international disputes. Law enforcement regimes. Law of armed conflict
Law of war and neutrality. Jus belli
Humanitarian law. Usus in bello
Intergovernmental congresses and conferences -- Continued
International Conference, Geneva, 1949
6454 Serials
6454.2 Monographs. By date
Diplomatic Conference on the Reaffirmation and Development of International Humanitarian Law, Applicable in Armed Conflicts, Geneva, 1974-1977
6456 Serials
6456.2 Monographs. By date
Hague International Conference on Humanitarian Assistance in Armed Conflict, 1988
For the Hague Peace Conferences see KZ6015+
6458 Serials
6458.2 Monographs. By date
6460.A-Z Other intergovernmental congresses and conferences. By name of congress, A-Z
Under each:
.xA12-.xA199 Serials
.xA3 Monographs. By date
Treaties and other international agreements. Conventions
6462 Collections. Selections
Multilateral treaties and conventions
Convention on Prohibition or Restrictions on the Use of Certain Conventional Weapons which may be deemed too excessiviely injurious or to have indiscriminate effects. Convention on Inhumane Weapons, 1981 see KZ5640.A12+
6464 Geneva Convention for the Amelioration of the Condition of Soldiers wounded in Armies in the Field. Geneva Convention, 1864 (Table K5)
6464.2 Geneva Convention for the Amelioration of the Condition of the Sick and Wounded of Armies in the Field, 1906 (Table K5)
International Convention relative to the Treatment of Prisoners of War, 1929 see KZ6490.2.A12+
6464.25 International Convention for the Amelioration of the Condition of the Wounded and Sick in Armies in the Field, 1929 (Table K5)
6464.3 Geneva Convention for the Amelioration of the Condition of the Wounded and Sick in Armed Forces in the Field, 1949 (Table K5)

Enforced settlement of international disputes. Law enforcement regimes. Law of armed conflict
Law of war and neutrality. Jus belli
Humanitarian law. Usus in bello
Treaties and other international agreements. Conventions
Multilateral treaties and conventions -- Continued
6464.4 Geneva Convention for the Amelioration of the Conditions of Wounded, Sick and Shipwrecked Members of the Armed Forces at Sea (including the Shipwrecked of Forced Aircraft Landings at Sea) (Table K5)
6465 Other treaties and conventions. By date of signature (Table K5)
6467 Non-governmental conferences. Symposia
e. g.
6467.E96 Roundtable of Experts on International Humanitarian Law Applicable to Armed Conflicts at Sea
6467.G68 Conference of Government Experts on the Reaffirmation and Development of International Humanitarian Law Applicable in Armed Conflicts
6469.A-Z Societies. Associations. Academies, etc. By name, A-Z
6469.H86 International Institute of Humanitarian Law
6471 General works
The wounded, shipwrecked and dead
Including works on the wounded and shipwrecked in maritime war and air warfare
6475 General works
6478 Special provisions for the treatment of the wounded
6478.5 Special provisions for treatment of the dead
Prisoners of war. Captivity
Intergovernmental congresses and conferences see KZ6450+
Treaties and other international agreements. Conventions
6490 Collections. Selections
Multilateral treaties and conventions
International Convention relative to the Treatment of Prisoners of War, 1929
6490.2.A12 Collections of miscellaneous materials. By date
Including selections of the treaty, official drafts, documents of advisory or research commissions, travaux preparatoires, etc.
6490.2.A15 Indexes and tables
Texts of, and works on, the treaty

Enforced settlement of international disputes. Law enforcement regimes. Law of armed conflict
Law of war and neutrality. Jus belli
Humanitarian law. Usus in bello
Prisoners of war. Captivity
Treaties and other international agreements. Conventions
Multilateral treaties and conventions
International Convention relative to the Treatment of Prisoners of War, 1929
Texts of, and works on, the treaty -- Continued

6490.2.A2 Unannotated editions. By date
Including official editions, with or without annotations

6490.2.A3-.Z39 Annotated editions. Commentaries. Works on the treaty
Including private drafts

Related agreements
Including accessions, protocols, successions, rectifications, concessions, schedules, annexed model treaties, bilateral treaties relating to nonregional multilateral treaty, etc.

6490.2.Z4 Collections. Selections

6490.2.Z5 Individual agreements. By date
e. g. Model agreement on repatriation and hospitalization of Prisoners of War, annexed to the convention, 1929

Miscellaneous documents of advisory or research commissions, etc. see KZ6490.2.A12

Works on the treaty see KZ6490.2.A3+

6490.2.Z8 Review conferences of the parties to the treaty. By date of the conference

6490.3 Geneva Convention Relative to the Treatment of Prisoners of War, 1949 (Table K5)

6490.4 Other treaties and conventions. By date of signature (Table K5)

6495 General works

6496 Captivity and termination of captivity

6497 Categories of persons considered POWs

6498 Disciplinary sanctions. Judicial proceedings

6500 Special provisions for treatment of prisoners of war

Hostages see KZ6517

Protection of civilians

Enforced settlement of international disputes. Law enforcement regimes. Law of armed conflict
Law of war and neutrality. Jus belli
Humanitarian law. Usus in bello
Protection of civilians -- Continued

6510.A-Z Intergovernmental congresses and conferences. By name of the congress, A-Z
Under each:
.xA12-.xA199 Serials
.xA3 Monographs. By date

Treaties and other international agreements. Conventions

6512 Collections. Selections

6512.2 Multilateral treaties and conventions. By date of signature

6512.2 1949 Geneva Convention on Protection of Civilian Persons in Time of War, 1949 (Table K5)

6515 General works

6517 Hostages
Cf. KZ7158 Hostage taking

6519 Treatment of internees in belligerent and occupied territories

6522 Treatment of civilian population in occupied territories
Including protection of sick and wounded civilians. Establishment of safety zones

Enemy aliens (at home) see K7205+

6530 Refugees. Population displacement. Forced migration

Warfare on sea. Naval warfare (Sea control)
Including naval air warfare, naval surface warfare, and submarine warfare

6540 Bibliography

Intergovernmental congresses and conferences. By name of the congress

London. International Naval Conference, 1908-1909

6545 Serials

6545.5 Monographs. By date

6547.A-Z Other congresses and conferences. By name of the congress, A-Z
Under each:
.xA12-.xA199 Serials
.xA3 Monographs. By date

Geneva. Conference for the Limitation of Naval Armament see KZ5615.C47

Treaties and other international agreements. Conventions

6548 Collections. Selections

Multilateral treaties and conventions

Enforced settlement of international disputes. Law enforcement regimes. Law of armed conflict
Law of war and neutrality. Jus belli
Warfare on sea. Naval warfare (Sea control)
Treaties and other international agreements. Conventions
Multilateral treaties and conventions -- Continued
6550 Declaration of Paris, 1856 (Table K5)
6550.2 Hague Convention (X. Adaptation of the Principles of the Geneva Convention to Maritime Warfare), 1907 (Table K5)
6552 Hague Convention (VII. Conversion of Merchantmen into Men-of-War), 1907 (Table K5)
6552.2 Hague Convention (VIII. Laying of Automatic Submarine Contact Mines), 1907 (Table K5)
6553 Hague Convention (XI. Status of Enemy Merchantmen at the Outbreak of Hostilities), 1907 (Table K5)
6554 Declaration of London, 1909 (Table K5)
Geneva Convention for the Amelioration of the Conditions of Wounded, Sick and Shipwrecked Members of Armed Forces at Sea (including the Shipwrecked of Forced Aircraft Landings at Sea) see KZ6464.4
6555 Other treaties and conventions. By date of signature (Table K5)
6560 Codification of law of sea warfare
Including history
For consolat de mar (Consulate of the Sea) see K1163.C6
6563 General works
6564 Blockade
Neutrality during sea warfare
6566 General works
6568 Doctrine of continuous voyage and transportation
6570 Unneutral service
Including transmission of intelligence, carriage of personnel for the enemy, and contraband of war
6572 Arming or converting merchant ships
For the Hague Convention VII see KZ6552
6573 Letters of marque (Privateering)
6574 Men-of-war. War vessels in neutral ports
6576 Visitation and capture of neutral vessels. Trial
6578 Right of visitation and search of vessel
Including convoy

Enforced settlement of international disputes. Law enforcement regimes. Law of armed conflict
Law of war and neutrality. Jus belli
Warfare on sea. Naval warfare (Sea control) -- Continued
6580 Capture. Seizure of enemy vessel
Including capture and seizure on the open sea or in the maritime territorial belt of the belligerents
For the Hague Convention XI. see KZ6553
Attack
6584 Immunity of vessels
Including mail boats, hospital and cartel ships, etc.
6586 Vessels in distress
Humanitarian law in maritime war. Wounded, shipwrecked, and dead see KZ6475+
Prize law
6590 Bibliography
6592.2 Treaties and other international agreements. Conventions. By date of signature
Declaration of London, 1909 see KZ6554
6595 Cases
General works. Treatises
6600 Early works to 1800
e.g. Hugo Grotius (1583-1645). De jure praedae
By language
European
6610 English
6613 French
6615 German
6617 Italian
6620 Spanish. Portuguese
Including Latin American works
6623 Scandinavian
6625 Other European (not A-Z)
6627 Asian and Middle Eastern
Including Arabic and Hebrew
Right of visitation, search capture of vessel see KZ6578
6633 Taking of vessel to the port of a prize court
Including conduct of neutral vessels
6636 Destruction of prizes
Including neutral prizes
Prize courts and procedure
6640 General works
Trial
6644 General works
6646 Burden of proof
6648 Trial of captured neutral vessel

Enforced settlement of international disputes. Law enforcement regimes. Law of armed conflict
Law of war and neutrality. Jus belli
Warfare on sea. Naval warfare (Sea control)
Prize law
Prize courts and procedure
Trial -- Continued
6650 Trial of captured aircraft
6655 Diplomatic protests and claims
6660.A-Z By region or country, A-Z
Air warfare (Air control)
6665 Bibliography
6668.A-Z Intergovernmental congresses and conferences. By name of the congress, A-Z
Under each:
.xA12-.xA199 *Serials*
.xA3 *Monographs. By date*
Treaties and other international agreements. Conventions
6670 Collections. Selections
6670.2 Multilateral treaties and conventions. By date of signature
Subarrange each by Table K5
Hague Declaration (prohibiting of projectiles or explosives from balloons and other air craft), 1899 see KZ5639
Codes of rules concerning aerial bombardment
6675 Air Warfare Rules (Hague Rules), 1923
6680 General works
6685 Air combat
Aerial bombardment
6695 General works
6697 Noncombatants. Civil population
Including dwellings
6700 Military targets. Fortifications. Ground forces
6710 Attacks on enemy civil aircraft
6714 Attacks on enemy merchant marine
Humanitarian law in air warfare see KZ6464.4
<6715> Space militarization. Warfare in outer space
see KZD6715
Special techniques of warfare
6718 Information warfare
The end of war. Armistice. Surrender. Postliminy
6730 Bibliography

Enforced settlement of international disputes. Law enforcement regimes. Law of armed conflict
Law of war and neutrality. Jus belli
The end of war. Armistice. Surrender. Postliminy -- Continued

6734.A-Z Intergovernmental congresses and conferences. By name of the congress, A-Z
Under each:
.xA12-.xA199 Serials
.xA3 Monographs. By date
e. g. Postdam Conference (of the Allied Powers in World War II), 1945

Treaties and other international agreements. Conventions
For peace treaties, collected and individual see KZ184+

6735 Collections. Selections

6735.2 Individual treaties and conventions. By date of signature
Subarrange individual treaties and conventions by Table K5
e. g.

6735.2 1943 Cairo Declaration, 1943 (Table K5)

6735.2 1945 Potsdam Declaration, 1945 (Table K5)

6740 Conferences. Symposia

6745 General works

6749 Cartels. Cartel ships

6753 Cessation of hostilities

6757 Truces and armistices
Including violation

6765 Postliminy
Including private and public property

6775 Post-hostility occupation of enemy territory. Post-surrender occupation

6785 Reparations and restitution. Demontages
Class here general works
For works on reparation, restitutions and demontages pertaining to a particular country, see the country, e. g. Germany, KK7642+

6795.A-Z Particular wars or conflicts, A-Z
For historical works about the war or conflict, see classes D, E, F
For trials of international crimes see KZ1190+

6795.A72 Arab-Israeli conflict
For Arab-Israeli conflict in Islamic law see KBP2418.I86

6795.C44 Chechni͡a Civil War, 1994-

Enforced settlement of international disputes. Law enforcement regimes. Law of armed conflict
Law of war and neutrality. Jus belli
Particular wars or conflicts, A-Z -- Continued
6795.E75 Eritrean-Ethiopian War, 1998-
6795.I7 Iran-Iraq War, 1980-1988
6795.I72 Iraq-Kuwait Crisis, 1990-1991
Including Persian Gulf War, 1991
6795.I73 Iraq War, 2003-
Israel-Arab Border Conflict, 1949- see KZ6795.A72
6795.K68 Kosovo Civil War, 1998-1999
6795.R83 Rwanda Civil War, 1994
6795.S53 Sierra Leone Civil War, 1991-
6795.S55 Sino-Japanese War, 1937-1945
6795.S65 Sri Lankan Civil War, 1983-2009
6795.T47 Terrorism, War on, 2001-2009
War on Terrorism, 2001-2009 see KZ6795.T47
6795.Y8 Yugoslav War, 1991-1995
International criminal law and procedure
Class here works on the body of rules and procedure designed to prohibit categories of conduct viewed as international crimes, as well as the principles and procedures governing the international investigation and prosecution of such crimes
7000 General. Comprehensive
Administration of international criminal justice see KZ7235
International criminal law
7011 Bibliography
7013 Annuals. Yearbooks
Associations. Societies. Academies, etc.
Class here works on individual learned societies and their activities
Including reports, bylaws, proceedings, directories, etc., and works about societies
7018.A-Z International. By name, A-Z
7020.A-Z National. By name, A-Z
e.g.
7020.G47 Gesellschaft für Völkerstrafrecht
7022.A-Z Intergovernmental congresses and conferences. By name, A-Z
Including proceedings, reports, resolutions, final acts, and works on the congress
Cf. KZ7259+ Congresses and conferences on the International Criminal Court
Sources
7025 Indexes. Digests
7026 Collections. Compilations. Selections

International criminal law and procedure
International criminal law
Sources -- Continued
7028 Treaties
Cf. KZ7288 Treaty establishing the International Criminal Court
Convention against Transnational Organized Crime (2003) see K5297.A42003
Convention on the Prevention and Punishment of the Crime of Genocide (1948) see KZ7180.A61948
Codes. Codifications
7030 Official
7032 Non-official
7033 Other
7034 Encyclopedias. Law dictionaries
7035 Directories
Trials by ad hoc tribunals see KZ1189.92+
7040 Legal research
Including the use of Web resources
7041 Legal education
7045 International Criminal Bar
7047 Conferences. Symposia
Including papers devoted to scholarly exploration of a subject
7050 General works. Treatises. History
Theory and principles of international criminal law
7052 Rule of law
7053 Judicial ethics
Cf. KZ7350 Code of Judicial Ethics
7054 Effectiveness and validity of law
7055 Application of the more favorable law
In dubio pro reo. Interpretation in favor of the accused see KZ7370
7058 Nulla poena, nullum crimen sine lege
Ne bis in idem. Double jeopardy see KZ7365
Statute of limitation see KZ7367
Scope and applicability of law
Including conflict of jurisdiction
Cf. KZ7383 Applicable law
7064 General works
7065 Retroactive law (ex post facto laws). Intertemporal law
7068 Precedents. Stare decisis
7070 Elements of international crimes
Including the definition and classification of international crimes
Criminal liability
7075 General works

International criminal law and procedure
International criminal law
Criminal liability -- Continued
7078 Mens rea. Dolus. Intent
Including knowledge
7080 Negligence
Including superior responsiblity
7085 Exemption from liability
Including capacity
Justification. Grounds for excluding criminal responsibility
7090 General works
7093.A-Z Particular grounds, A-Z
7093.D87 Duress and threats
7093.N43 Necessity
7093.S45 Self-defense
7093.S87 Superior orders
Forms of crime and criminal responsibility
Including completion and attempt, principals and accessories, collective crimes, etc.
7094 General works
7095 Command responsibility
Punishment and penalties
7098 General works
7105.A-Z Particular penalties, A-Z
Sentencing. Determination of sentence
Including circumstances influencing the measure of punishment
7110 General works
7118 Aggravating circumstances
7120 Extenuating circumstances
7122 Reduction of sentence
Causes barring prosecution or execution of punishment
7128 General works
7130 Amnesty. Pardon
7135 Statute of limitation. Limitation of action
International crimes or groups of crimes
Cf. KZ1168+ Trials of international crimes
7139 General works
7140 Aggression. Crimes against peace (Table KZ12)
Crimes against humanity. War crimes
7145 General works
Particular crimes
7147 Apartheid (Table KZ12)
Treaties and other international agreements. Conventions
7147.A6<date> Multilateral treaties

International criminal law and procedure
International criminal law
International crimes or groups of crimes
Crimes against humanity. War crimes
Particular crimes
Apartheid
Treaties and other international agreements. Conventions
Multilateral treaties -- Continued

7147.A61966 International Convention on the Elimination of All Forms of Racial Discrimination (1966) (Table K5)

7150 Deportation or forcible transfer of population
Including forced relocation during armed conflict or internal strife (communal violence)

7152 Enforced disappearance

7154 Forcible conscription of child soldiers under the age of fifteen

7155 Trafficking in persons. Enslavement (Table KZ12)
For human trafficking see K5297
For human smuggling see K5299

7158 Hostage taking
For the Geneva law see KZ6517

7162 Sexual violence as a weapon of war
Including rape, sexual slavery, forced prostitution, forced pregnancy, forced sterilization

7166 Employing poisons or poisoned weapons. Employing weapons or projectiles causing superfluous suffering

7170 Torture or inhuman treatment. Biological experiments (Table KZ12)
Treaties and other international agreements. Conventions

7170.A6<date> Multilateral treaties

7170.A61985 Convention against Torture and Other Cruel, Inhuman or Degrading Treatment or Punishment (1985) (Table K5)

7175 Vandalism. Destruction of the cultural heritage of racial, ethnic, cultural, religious, or social groups (Table KZ12)
Treaties and other international agreements. Conventions

7175.A6<date> Multilateral treaties

7175.A61954 Convention for the Protection of Cultural Property in the Event of Armed Conflict (1954) (Table K5)

7177.A-Z Other crimes against humanity or war crimes, A-Z

International criminal law and procedure
International criminal law
International crimes or groups of crimes -- Continued
Genocide
7180 General (Table KZ12)
Treaties and other international agreements. Conventions
7180.A6<date> Multilateral treaties
7180.A61948 Convention on the Prevention and Punishment of the Crime of Genocide (1948) (Table K5)
7188.A-Z Special topics, A-Z
7192 Offenses against the administration of justice (International Criminal Court)
Other crimes under international law
Class here crimes not listed in the Rome Statute of the International Criminal Court, but covered by other conventions
7198 General works
Particular crimes
7200 International environmental offenses
7205 Drug trafficking
7212 Piracy at sea (Table KZ12)
Terrorism
Including counter-terrorism
7220 General (Table KZ12)
7225.A-Z Special topics, A-Z
7225.B56 Biological weapons
7225.W43 Weapons of mass destruction
International criminal courts
For trials by international courts and criminal tribunals associated with particular wars or conflicts, e.g. the International Criminal Tribunal for the Former Yugoslavia, see the war or conflict at KZ1191+
7230 General works
Including comparative works on ad hoc tribunals and international criminal courts
7235 Administration of international criminal justice
International cooperation. Judicial assistance see KZ7480
7240 Hybrid criminal courts
For trials by the Hybrid criminal courts see KZ1189.92+
International Criminal Court (2002 -)
7250 Bibliography
7255 Yearbooks
7257 Official Journal
Intergovernmental congresses and conferences
Including proceedings, reports, resolutions, final acts, and works on the congress

International criminal law and procedure
International criminal courts
International Criminal Court (2002 -)
Intergovernmental congresses and conferences -- Continued
7259 Collective
Preparatory commissions and committees
7260 General
7263 Ad Hoc Committee on the Establishment of an International Criminal Court
7266 International Law Commission
7270 United Nations Diplomatic Conference of Plenipotentiaries on the Establishment of an International Criminal Court (1998 : Rome, Italy)
7274.A-Z Other intergovernmental congresses and conferences. By name, A-Z
Treaties and other international agreements. Basic documents
7280 Indexes and tables. Digests
7284 Collections. Selections
7288 Rome Statute of the International Criminal Court (Table K5)
Adopted in 1998; entered into force in 2002
7290.A-Z Bilateral treaties. By first named country (alphabetically), A-Z
Subarrange treaties of each country by date of signature
Further subarrange each treaty by Table K6
Reports. Judgments
7295 Indexes
7297 Digests. Summary of judgments
7298 Advisory opinions and orders
General collections. Selections
With or without pleadings
7300 Serials
7303 Monographs. By date
Pleadings. Oral arguments. Documents
7308 Collections
7310 Individual documents
Trials see KZ1215+
7311 Conferences. Symposia
Including papers devoted to scholarly exploration of the subject
7312 General. History
Including legitimacy and legal capacity
Organization and administration
For the Rome Statute of the International Criminal Court see KZ7288

International criminal law and procedure
International criminal courts
International Criminal Court (2002 -)
Organization and administration -- Continued
General works see KZ7312
7320 Assembly of States Parties to the Rome Statute of the International Criminal Court
Class here works on management oversight and legislative activity of this body

Organs of the court
7325 General works
7328 Presidency. President
Including elections, function, and powers
7332 Prosecutor and Deputy Prosecutor
Including disqualification
7336 Registrar and Deputy Registrar
7340 Judges. Presiding judges
Including disqualification
7346 Privileges and immunities
7350 Codes
Including the Code of Judicial Ethics and the Code of Professional Conduct for Counsel
7355 Rules and regulations of the court
Including finance, staff, records, etc.
7360-7480 Procedure
7360 General works
Including comparative works on the rules of procedure and evidence of international courts and ad hoc tribunals
Procedural principles
7363 Admissability or inadmissability of case
7364 Fair trial
7365 Double jeopardy. Ne bis in idem
7367 Statute of limitation. Limitation of action
7370 In dubio pro reo. Interpretation in favor of the accused
Jurisdiction and venue
Including challenge of jurisdiction
7375 General works
7377 Universal jurisdiction
7379 Complementarity. Concurrent jurisdiction
7383 Applicable law
7387 Information. Confidentiality of information
Including protection of national security information
7390 Investigation and prosecution. Indictment
Including duty of prosecutors and preliminary ruling on admissibility of case
Compulsory measures against the accused. Arrest and surrender. Detention

International criminal law and procedure
International criminal courts
Procedure
Compulsory measures against the accused. Arrest and surrender. Detention -- Continued
7394 General works
7396 Habeas corpus
7398 Extradition
7400 Charges
7405 Rights of suspects and detainees. Protection of human rights
Defense. Legal representation. Legal aid
7408 General works
7410 Public Counsel for Defense
Including counsel-client privilege and privileged communications
7414 Pre-trial. Pre-Trial Chamber
Including constitution of Pre-Trial Chamber
Trial. Trial Chamber
Including constitution of the Trial Chamber
For trials of international crimes see KZ1215+
7418 General works
Evidence. Burden of proof
Including admission and disclosure of evidence
7422 General works
7424 Testimony. Witnesses
Including self-incrimination of witnesses
7428 Expert witnesses
7430 Admission of guilt. Plea bargaining
7434 Misconduct and disruption of proceedings
Judicial decisions. Judgments
Cf. KZ7295+ Reports of decisions
7438 General works
7440 Conviction or acquittal
Remedies
7444 General works
7448 Appeal. Appeal Chamber. Revision
Including appeal proceedings
Execution of sentence. Enforcement
7450 General works
7453 Capital punishment
7455 Imprisonment
7458 Fines
7460 Order of forfeiture
7464 Reparations to victims
7470.A-Z Other penalties, A-Z
7474 Transfer of sentenced person to state of enforcement

International criminal law and procedure
International criminal courts
Procedure -- Continued
7476 Parole. Amnesty
7480 International judicial assistance
Including agreements and forms of cooperation
Proceedings relating to particular subjects or governed by special rules
7484 General works
7490.A-Z Special topics, A-Z
7490.P43 Peacekeepers
Victims of crimes
Including victims' rights and legal representation
Cf. KZ7464 Reparations to victims
7495 General works
7500 Trust Fund for Victims

Law of the sea
Class here works on the international regime of the oceans (High seas regime)
Including works on both international public and commercial maritime law combined
1002 Bibliography
1006 Periodicals
1021 Annuals. Yearbooks
e. g.
Annuario de derecho maritimo
1022 Monographic series
1024 Societies. Associations. Academies, etc.
Including reports, bylaws, proceedings, directories, etc. and works about a society
Intergovernmental congresses and conferences
Including serial congresses, and ad hoc conferences of heads of state
For other conferences see KZA1141
United Nations conferences
For UN documents (Sales publications) see JZ5090+
United Nations Conference on the Law of the Sea, 1958
1040 Serials
1041 Monographs. By date
Second United Nations Conference on the Law of the Sea, 1960
1043 Serials
1044 Monographs. By date
Third United Nations Conference on the Law of the Sea, 1973-1982
1046 Serials
1047 Monographs. By date
1065.A-Z Other congresses and conferences. By name of the congress, A-Z
Under each:
.xA12-.xA199 Serials
.xA3 Monographs. By date
Treaties and other international agreements. Conventions
1118 Indexes and tables. Digests
1120 Collections. Selections
Including either multilateral or bilateral treaties, or both
Multilateral treaties and conventions
1120.2 Convention on the High Seas, 1958 (Table K5)
1120.3 UN Convention on the Law of the Sea, 1982 (Table K5)
1120.4 Agreement relating to the Implementation of Part XI of the UN Convention on the Law of the Sea, 1994 (Table K5)
1121 Other treaties and conventions. By date of signature (Table K5)

Treaties and other international agreements. Conventions -- Continued

1122.A-Z Bilateral treaties. By country, A-Z

Subarrange treaties of each country by date of signature. Further subarrange each treaty by Table K5

Decisions. Administrative rulings. Reports

1123 Indexes and tables. Digests. By date

1123.5 Serials

1124 Monographs. By date

1125 Dictionaries. Encyclopedias

1141 Conferences. Symposia

1145 General works

Including early works

e. g. Molloy, Charles, 1646-1690, De jure maritimo et navali; or, a treatise of affairs maritime and of commerce (1676)

1146.A-Z By region or country, A-Z

<1150-1188> Commercial maritime law and admiralty

see K1150+

<1195-1223> Maritime social legislation

see K1195+

KZA

Concepts and principles

Including historic concepts

General works see KZA1145

1340 Mare clausum doctrine. Dominion of the Sea. Maritime sovereignty. Dominium maris

Including early works

e. g. Selden, John, 1584-1654. Mare clausum; Bijnkershoek, Cornelis van, 1673-1743. De dominio maris

Mare liberum doctrine. Freedom of the high seas. Res communes

Including freedom of navigation, fishing, freedom to lay submarine cables and pipelines, freedom to fly over the high seas, etc.

1348 General works. Treatises

Including early works

e. g. Grotius, Hugo, 1583-1645. Mare liberum

Reasonable use theory. Regulated use. Commons regimes for exploration and exploitation of res communes

Including the high seas, deep-sea bed (ocean bottom) and its subsoil

For prohibition of the emplacement of nuclear weapons of mass destruction on the sea-bed, ocean floor and subsoil thereof see KZ5715.2+

1370 General (Table K8)

Free access regime

1375 General (Table K8)

Regime for the high-seas fisheries

Concepts and principles
Mare liberum doctrine. Freedom of the high seas. Res communes
Reasonable use theory. Regulated use. Commons regimes for exploration and exploitation of res communes
Free access regime
Regime for the high-seas fisheries -- Continued
General works see K3886+
Principle of freedom of fishing see KZA3896
Common heritage of mankind regime over the ocean bottom and its subsoil
For marine resources (conservation and development) see KZA3481+
1390 General (Table K8)
International Sea Bed Authority
1400 General works (Table K8)
1403 Organs of the Sea-Bed Authority
1405 International legal status (legal personality). Jurisdiction
1410 The source of law of the sea
Class here works on international customs, treaty law and other official acts, principes généraux, codes, etc. as the basis of law of the sea
1415 Legal hermeneutics. Interpretation and construction
For general works on legal regimes governing common spaces (International commons) see KZ1321
For comparative analysis of common principles in law and legal regimes governing the high seas, sea bed, space and Antarctica combined see KZ1322+
1417 Legal semantics. Terminology. Definitions
Maritime boundaries. Delimitation of sea areas. National claims to marine areas (Maritime zones)
Treaties and other international agreements. Conventions
1430 Indexes. Tables. Digests
1435 Collections. Selections
Including either multilateral or bilateral treaties, or both
1440.2 Multilateral treaties and conventions. By date of signature
Subarrange each by Table K5
e. g. Convention of the Territorial Sea and the Contiguous Zone, 1958
1442.A-Z Bilateral treaties. By country, A-Z
Subarrange treaties of each country by date of signature. Further subarrange each treaty by Table K5
1450 General works

Maritime boundaries. Delimitation of sea areas. National claims to marine areas (Maritime zones) -- Continued

1460 Baseline delimitation. Low and high water lines. Lines of demarcation

Including straights' baselines, archipelagic baselines, bays, and delimitation from various offshore structures (man-made islands, lighthouses, etc.) and ports

Coastal (littoral) state and port state. Authority and jurisdiction

1470 General (Table K8)

1500 Regime of internal waters. Authority of the coastal state and port state over internal waters

Including control over entry of foreign vessels or by alleged right of innocent passage, and access to ports

Regime of territorial sea (marginal sea) and high seas areas contiguous to the territorial sea (special contiguous zones)

Class here works on territorial sovereignty (authority) over territorial waters (width and breadth of the territorial maritime belt) and on special jurisdiction marine areas, e.g. the 3 to 12 miles zones and 200 miles zone; and on the authority to control or exclude passage and navigation in the marginal belt, exploitation of animal and mineral resources, etc.

Including authority over straits, and including the ocean bottom and its subsoil

1540 General (Table K8)

1545 Archipelagic waters. Claim of authority over archipelagic waters by archipelagic states

1550 Doctrine of innocent passage and navigation within the maritime belt

1555 Rights of access of land-locked states to and from the sea. Freedom of transit

Exclusive fishery and economic zones

Including attributed rights, coastal state in the zone, and including conflict resolution

For principle of freedom of fishing see KZA3896

1560 General (Table K8)

Environmental protection in the exclusive economic zone see K3591

Continental shelf. Outer continental shelf. Submarine areas contiguous to the coast and legal continental shelf

Including the subsoil

Treaties and other international agreements. Conventions

1630 Indexes. Tables. Digests

1635 Collections. Selections

Including either multilateral or bilateral treaties, or both

Maritime boundaries. Delimitation of sea areas. National claims to marine areas (Maritime zones)
Continental shelf. Outer continental shelf. Submarine areas contiguous to the coast and legal continental shelf
Treaties and other international agreements. Conventions -- Continued
1640.2 Multilateral treaties and conventions. By date of signature
Subarrange each by Table K5
e. g. Convention on the Continental Shelf, 1958
1642.A-Z Bilateral treaties and conventions. By country, A-Z
Subarrange treaties of each country by date of signature.
Further subarrange each treaty by Table K5
1660 General works
1662 Decisions (Collected. Selected)
1664 Conferences. Symposia
Subsoil beneath the bed of the open sea see KZA1390+
Particular oceans and high seas areas
1667 Arctic Ocean
1669 Caribbean Area
1670 Indian Ocean
1672 Southern Ocean (Antarctic waters)
Legal regimes of enclosed or semi-enclosed seas
1686 General (Table K8)
Particular seas or sea areas
1686.5 Aegean Sea
1686.7 Aqaba, Gulf of
1687 Baltic Sea
1687.3 Bengal, Bay of
1687.5 Caspian Sea
1688 Mediterranean Sea
1690 Persian-Arab Gulf
1692 South China Sea
1693 Thailand, Gulf of
1694 Yellow Sea
Marine resources conservation and development
Including the territorial sea
<3481-3485.4> General
see K3481+
<3485.7> Marine mineral resources (including in the subsoil of the deep sea-bed and continental shelf minerals)
see K3485.7
High-seas fisheries see K3886+
Marine pollution
Including environmental protection of the territorial sea
<3586-3590.4> General
see K3586+

Marine resources conservation and development
Marine pollution -- Continued
<3591> Land-based marine pollution
see K3591
Vessel source pollution of the sea. Pollution from off-shore installations
Including pollution from the air
<3591.2> General
see K3591.2
<3592> Oil pollution
see K3592
Cf. K956 Liability for oil pollution damage
<3592.5> Waste disposal in the ocean
see K3592.5
For radioactive waste disposal see K3592.6
<3592.6> Radioactive pollution of the sea
see K3592.6
<3592.9> Pollution control zones
High-seas fisheries and fisheries regimes. International fishery management
Class here works on the present status and prospects of the regime governing the high-seas fisheries
<3891-3895.6> General
see K3891+
3896 Principle of freedom of fishing
Cf. KZA1560+ Exclusive fishery and economic zones
<3896.5> Intergovernmental conservation and management regimes
For conservation and management of a particular species see K3900.A+
<3897> General
see K3897
Treaties and other international agreements. Conventions
Multilateral treaties and conventions. By date of signature
<3897.A41958> Convention on Fishing and Conservation of Living Resources of the High Seas, 1958
see K3897.A41958

Marine resources conservation and development
High-seas fisheries and fisheries regimes. International fishery management -- Continued
<3898.A-Z> High-seas fisheries conservation zones and regions, A-Z
Including international conventions and global as well as regional organizations concerned with high-seas fisheries, e. g. International Commission for the North West Atlantic Fisheries; North East Atlantic Fisheries Commission; etc.
For regional and country fisheries in general, as well as regional and country fisheries for a particular species, see the subclass for the region or country, e. g. Antarctica, KWX795+
For high seas fisheries for a particular species see K3900.A+
<3898.M54> Middle Atlantic
<3898.N65> North Atlantic
<3898.N654> North-East Atlantic
<3898.N66> North Pacific
<3898.N67> Northwest Atlantic
<3898.S68> South Pacific
<3900.A-Z> Special fish or marine fauna, A-Z
<3900.H35> Halibut
Krill see KWX813.K85
<3900.S43> Seals
<3900.T84> Tuna
<3900.W57> Whales
Public order of the oceans
4130 General (Table K8)
Water transportation. Navigation and shipping see K4150+
<4150> General works
<4150.2> International Maritime Organization (IMO)
Previously Intergovernmental Maritime Consultative Organization
Class here works on the legal aspects of the International Maritime Organization
For works issued by the International Maritime Organization, see the appropriate subject
For administrative material see HE561.5
For its Maritime Safety Committee see K4166
For technical materials see VK1+
Merchant mariners see K1196+
Ships
<4157> Nationality of ships
Maritime flag. Territory of the flag
4158 General works
4158.5 Verification of the flag

Public order of the oceans
Water transportation. Navigation and shipping
Ships
Maritime flag. Territory of the flag -- Continued
Right to visit, search, and arrest of the vessel see KZ6578
4159 Ships papers. Registry
Safety regulations. Inspection
<4161-4165.6> General
<4166> Maritime Safety Committee of the Intergovernmental Maritime Consultative Organization
<4168> Manning requirements
<4170> Load line
<4174> Tonnage measurement
<4176.A-Z> Special types of vessels, A-Z
<4176.N83> Nuclear ships
<4176.O33> Offshore support vessels
<4176.P55> Pleasure craft. Yachts
<4178.A-Z> Special types of cargo, A-Z
<4178.D36> Dangerous articles
<4178.G73> Grain
Lumber see KZA4178.T56
<4178.T56> Timber. Lumber
<4180.A-Z> Special topics, A-Z
<4180.D57> Diving systems
Electrical installations see KZA4180.M33
<4180.F57> Fire and fire prevention
<4180.M33> Machinery and electrical installations
<4180.P47> Pesticides
Navigation and pilotage
Including coastwise navigation
<4182> General works
<4184> Rules of the road at sea
Inland navigation. Inland waterways
<4188> General works
<4189> Rivers
<4194> International waterways
Collision at sea. Shipwreck. Salvage see K1188.A8
Harbors and ports
<4198> General works
<4200> Port charges. Tonnage fees
Offshore structures. Artificial islands
Including installations for exploration and exploitation of natural resources, e. g. drilling platforms
<4204> General works
<4205> Lighthouses
International Tribunal of the Law of the Sea

International Tribunal of the Law of the Sea -- Continued
5200 General works
5205 Organization. Statute. Documents

Space law. Law of outer space

Class here works on the legal regimes of space, outer space, the moon and other celestial bodies

Including works on both international public and commercial law of space and outer space

1002 Bibliography

1006 Periodicals

1021 Annuals. Yearbooks

e. g.

Annuaire de droit aérien et spatial. Yearbook of air and space law

1022 Monographic series

1024 Societies. Associations. Academies, etc. for the study and development of space law. By name

Including reports, bylaws, proceedings, directories, etc., and works about a society

e. g. International Institute of Space Law

Intergovernmental congresses and conferences

Including standing (serial) conferences and ad hoc conferences

For other congresses and conferences see KZD1141

United Nations conferences

For UN documents (Sales publications) see JZ5090

First United Nations Conference on the Exploration and Peaceful Uses of Outer Space, 1968

1040 Serials

1041 Monographs. By date

Second United Nations Conference on Space Applications

1044 Serials

1045 Monographs. By date

1065.A-Z Other congresses and conferences. By name of the congress, A-Z

Under each:

.xA12-.xA199	*Serials*
.xA3	*Monographs. By date*

Treaties and other international agreements. Conventions

1118 Indexes and tables. Digests

1120 Collections. Selections

Including multilateral or bilateral treaties, or both

Multilateral treaties and conventions

1121 Treaty on Principles Governing the Activities of States in the Exploration and Use of Outer Space, including the Moon and other Celestial Bodies. Outer Space Treaty, 1967 (Table K5)

Agreement on the Rescue of Astronauts, the Return of Astronauts and the Return of Objects launched into Outer Space, 1968 see KZD4320.2 1968

Treaties and other international agreements. Conventions
Multilateral treaties and conventions -- Continued
Convention on International Liability for Damages caused by Space Objects, 1972 see KZD4402.2 1972
International Telecommunication Convention, 1973 see K4296+
Convention on Registration of Objects launched into Outer Space, 1975 see KZD4152.2
Declaration of Bogota, 1976 see KZD3490.2
1121.2 Agreement Governing the Activities of States on the Moon and other Celestial Bodies. Moon Treaty, 1979 (Table K5)
1121.3 Other treaties and agreements. By date of signature (Table K5)
1122.A-Z Bilateral treaties and conventions. By country, A-Z
Subarrange treaties of each country by date of signature. Further subarrange each treaty by Table K5
1125 Dictionaries. Encyclopedias
1141 Conferences. Symposia
1145 General works
1146.A-Z Position of legislative or executive branch on space law. By country, A-Z
Relation to other disciplines and topics
1147 Astronomers and space law
1148 Sacred space (Canon law)
1149.A-Z Other, A-Z
Concepts and principles. Theory
Class here works on the theory, development and formulation of space law
Including works on the contributions of IGOs and NGOs to the theory of law of space
General works see KZD1145
Domain of space law. Universal and regional application
1340 General works
1344 Subjects of space law
Including states and intergovernmental organizations
1348 Freedom of space exploration and exploitation
Including discovery, acquisitioning, capture, occupation, space colonization, etc.

Concepts and principles. Theory -- Continued
Regulated use theory. Commons regimes for exploration and exploitation of space, the moon, celestial bodies and natural resources thereof
Including non-appropriation (national) of celestial bodies and their resources
Including common heritage of mankind regime and free access to the commons regime
For the concepts of legal regimes governing the international commons in general see KZ1322+
1390 General
1400 International space authority
1410 The source of the law of space
Class here works on international customs, treaty law and other official acts, principes généraux, codes, etc. as the basis of the law of space
Including the work of the United Nations, the ICAO and other UN bodies and programs
1415 Legal hermeneutics. Interpretation and construction
For general works on legal regimes governing common spaces (International commons) see KZ1321
For comparative analysis of common principles in law and legal regimes governing the high seas, sea bed, space and Antarctica combined see KZ1322
1417 Legal semantics. Terminology. Definitions
Boundaries. Demarcation and delimitation of outer space
1420 Bibliography
Treaties and other international agreements. Conventions
1430 Indexes and tables. Digests
1435 Collections. Selections
1440.2 Multilateral treaties and conventions. By date of signature
Subarrange each by Table K5
Airspace and outer space (Distinction)
For airspace in private law see K740+
1445 General works
1447 Sovereignty. Jurisdiction
Including questions of extra-territorial supremacy
1453 Aerospace continuum
1455 Doctrine of innocent passage of spacecraft through airspace (Intrusion)
Peaceful uses of outer space. International cooperation
Class here works on exploration and structured utilization of the spatial area and its resources
3489 General (Table K8)

Peaceful uses of outer space. International cooperation -- Continued
Space resources. Conservation and development regimes
Including the moon and other celestial bodies and their resource on surface, subsurface and their geostationary orbit, etc.; and including such resources as solar energy
Treaties and other international agreements. Conventions
3489.5 Indexes. Tables. Digests
3490 Collections. Selections
3490.2 Multilateral treaties and conventions. By date of signature
Subarrange each by Table K5
e. g. Bogota Declaration (relating to Sovereignty of Equatorial States over the corresponding Segments of the Geostationary Orbit), 1976
3491 General works
3491.5 Natural resources. Nomenclature
Space environment. Environmental impact of activities in outer space
3598 General (Table K8)
3599 Environmental planning. Conservation of natural resources
Space pollution. Pollution of the geostationary orbit
Including environmental control
3600 General (Table K8)
Pollutants or hazardous processes
3602 General (Table K8)
3604 Harmful experiments
3608 Space debris
Public order in space and outer space. Order of conduct
4030 General (Table K8)
4050 Control of space industrialization and commercial activities in outer space
Space flight. Navigation and pilotage (Astronautics)
Including military astronautics
4080 General (Table K8)
<4091-4124> Regulation of civil aviation (commercial aeronautics)
see K4091+
4130 Astronauts
Space vehicles. Space shuttles. Launch vehicles
4140 General (Table K8)
4145 Nationality. Registration of space vehicles
Including space ships with international crews, and of international operating agency
International registration and notification of launches
Treaties and other international agreements. Conventions
4150 Indexes. Tables. Digests

Peaceful uses of outer space. International cooperation
Public order in space and outer space. Order of conduct
Space flight. Navigation and pilotage (Astronautics)
Space vehicles. Space shuttles. Launch vehicles
International registration and notification of launches
Treaties and other international agreements. Conventions -- Continued

4152 Collections. Selections

4152.2 Multilateral treaties and conventions. By date of signature
Subarrange each by Table K5
e. g. Convention on Registration of Objects launched into Outer Space, 1975

4160 General works

4165 Space stations. Space laboratories. Legal (international) status
Including manned space stations

Safety regulations of space flight

4170 General (Table K8)

4180 Operational soundness of spacecraft

4190 Space centers. Space ports

4192 Tracking of space flights

4200 Reciprocal inspection of space stations, labs, installations, etc.

4210 Navigation and pilotage (Astronautics)

Space communication. Artificial satellites in telecommunication

<4301-4305.6> General
see K4301+

<4303.31973> International Telecommunication Convention, 1973
see K4303.3+

<4307> Earth stations. Geostationary satellites

<4308> Allocation of frequency bands
see K4308

Particular uses or functions of satellites

4310 Artificial satellites in navigation

Artificial satellites in earth sciences see K3479

Satellite solar power stations see K3992

Metereological satellites see K3775.W4

Artificial satellites in remote sensing see KZD5632

Rescue operations in outer space
Including astronauts and objects launched into outer space

Treaties and other international agreements. Conventions

4320.2 Multilateral treaties and conventions. By date of signature (Table K5)
e. g.

Peaceful uses of outer space. International cooperation
Public order in space and outer space. Order of conduct
Rescue operations in outer space
Treaties and other international agreements. Conventions
Multilateral treaties and conventions. By date of signature -- Continued
Agreement on the Rescue of Astronauts, the Return of Astronauts and the Return of Objects launched into Outer Space, 1968
4326 General works
Liability for accidents
4400 Indexes. Tables. Digests
4402 Collections. Selections
Treaties and other international agreements. Conventions
4402.2 Multilateral treaties and conventions. By date of signature (Table K5)
e. g.
Convention on International Liability for Damages caused by Space Objects, 1972
4404 General works
4406 Scope of application
Including liability of state of registry; liability of launching authority; liability of operator of space vehicle; liability of international organization; etc.
For products liability in general see K953+
For government tort liability and liability of international organizations in general see K967
Claims settled by an ad hoc tribunal or claims commissions see KZ221+
Un-peaceful uses of outer space. Militarization and military supremacy in outer space
5614 Bibliography
Intergovernmental congresses and conferences
Including standing (serial) conferences and ad hoc conferences
<5615> Conference on Disarmament, 1978
see KZ5615.C55
5616.A-Z Other congresses and conferences. By name of congress, A-Z
Under each:
.xA12-.xA199 *Serials*
.xA3 *Monographs. By date*
Treaties and other international agreements. Conventions
5620 Indexes. Tables. Digests
5622 Collections. Selections

Un-peaceful uses of outer space. Militarization and military supremacy in outer space
Treaties and other international agreements. Conventions -- Continued
5622.2 Multilateral treaties and conventions. By date of signature (Table K5)
e. g.
Treaty on Principles Governing the Activities of States in the Exploration and Use of Outer Space (Article IV), including the Moon and other Celestial Bodies. Outer Space Treaty, 1967 see KZD1121
Treaty on Open Skies, 1992 see KZ5885.2
5624 Conferences. Symposia
5625 General works
5632 Intelligence activities in outer space. Space surveillance. Reconnaissance satellites
Including works on satellite monitoring
Disarmament and demilitarization regimes in outer space. Limitation of use and ban of weapons. Prevention of arms race
Including nuclear (strategic) weapons, orbital weapons of mass destruction, installations of such weapons on celestial bodies, and military use of nuclear energy in general
Bibliography see KZD5614
5648.A-Z Intergovernmental congresses and conferences. By name of the congress, A-Z
Under each:
.xA12-.xA199 *Serials*
.xA3 *Monographs. By date*
Including standing (serial) conferences and ad hoc conferences
Treaties and other international agreements. Conventions
5648.52 Indexes. Tables. Digests
5649 Collections. Selections
5650.2 Multilateral treaties and conventions. By date of signature (Table K5)
5652 General works
Cessation of nuclear weapon tests in the atmosphere and outer space
Treaties and other international agreements. Conventions
5675 Indexes. Tables. Digests
5677 Collections. Selections
5680.2 Multilateral treaties and conventions. By date of signature (Table K5)
e. g.

Un-peaceful uses of outer space. Militarization and military supremacy in outer space

Disarmament and demilitarization regimes in outer space. Limitation of use and ban of weapons. Prevention of arms race

Cessation of nuclear weapon tests in the atmosphere and outer space

Treaties and other international agreements. Conventions

Multilateral treaties and conventions. By date of signature -- Continued

Treaty Banning Nuclear Weapon tests in the Atmosphere, in Outer Space and under Water. Test Ban Treaty, 1963 see KZ5680

5695 General works

Nuclear weapon free zone. International commons as zones of peace see KZ5687+

6374 Threat of force. Self-defense in outer space

6715 Warfare in outer space and neutrality

Table KZ1 has been replaced by Table K23

Table KZ2 has been replaced by Table K24

Table KZ3 has been replaced by Table K1

Table KZ4 has been replaced by Table K2

Table KZ5 has been replaced by Table K3

TABLES

Table KZ6 has been replaced by Table K4

Table KZ7 has been replaced by Table K5

Table KZ8 has been replaced by Table K6

Table KZ9 has been replaced by Table K8

TABLES

.A12A-.A12Z Court rules and procedure. General works on the court

.A2A-.A2Z General (Collected)

Including judgments, opinions, digests, etc.

.A3-.Z9 Individual trials. by first named defendant or best known (popular) name

Subarrange each by Table K2

.xA12-.xA199	Court rules and procedure. General works on the court
.xA2-.xA299	General (Collected) Including judgments, opinions, digests, etc.
.xA3-.xZ9	Individual trials. By first named defendant or best known (popular) name

.A2 Bibliography

.A3 Periodicals

Including gazettes, yearbooks, bulletins, etc.

Treaties and other international agreements. Conventions

.A4 Indexes. Digests

.A5 Collections. Selections

Including either multilateral or bilateral treaties, or both

.A6<date> Multilateral treaties

Arrange chronologically by appending the date of signature of the treaty to this number and deleting any trailing zeros. Subarrange further by Table K5

.A7A-.A7Z Bilateral treaties. By country, A-Z

Subarrange by date of signature

For bilateral treaties relating to nonregional multilateral treaties see KZ12 .A6<date>

Opinions. Recommendations see KZ12 .A9+

.A8 Conferences. Symposia

.A9-.Z9 General works. Treatises

Including opinions, recommendations, consultations, studies, etc.

A

B

INDEX

INDEX

E

J

M

P

Q

R

S

U

V

W

GPO U.S. GOVERNMENT PRINTING OFFICE: 2012–372–396/40011